PRAISE FOR JACQUELINE PIRTLE

"Jacqueline takes you always directly to what you are ready to see or experience."

— LONGTIME CLIENT AND READER

"It is liberating to face your own blocks and to be finally free of the weight that they have caused for many years. And while for me the changes I'm experiencing are noticeable and real, I still feel like myself. Just a more sure self."

— LONGTIME CLIENT AND READER

"Jacqueline makes me BELIEVE I can be and live a joyful and magical existence every new day of my life!"

— LONGTIME CLIENT AND READER

JACQUELINE PIRTLE

I'd give anything for...

Express your manifestations

Copyright © 2024 Jacqueline Pirtle
www.FreakyHealer.com

All rights reserved. No part of this book may be reproduced or transmitted in any form or by any means, electronic or mechanical, including photocopying, recording, or by any information storage and retrieval system without the written permission of the publisher, except where permitted by law.

ISBN-13: 978-1-955059-63-3

Publisher: Freaky Healer

Editor-in-chief: Zoe Pirtle
Book cover design by Kingwood Creations kingwoodcreations.com

Author photo courtesy of Lionel Madiou madious.com

Dear amazing manifester,

As a holistic practitioner, spiritual energy healer, energetic living and businessing expert, and emotional intelligence teacher I have written over 17 books for adults and children, supporting people to live a more conscious, mindful, and happier life. You can find out more at www.freakyhealer.com and on my Amazon Author Page.

Thank you for purchasing this journal. I truly hope you enjoy it as much as I loved writing it. If so, could you take a short minute and leave a review on Amazon.com and Goodreads.com as soon as you can? Your kind feedback helps other readers find my books more easily, and manifest faster. Consider it a happy deed for the world. Thank you!

Happiest,
Jacqueline

ACKNOWLEDGMENTS

Let's be honest here… I have a dream team!

I could not have finished this book without the help of talented, creative, manifesting, and phenomenal professionals.

From the bottom of my heart, I want to thank Zoe Pirtle for her editorial mastery; kingwoodcreations.com for their fun and polished book cover design; and madiouART.com for an amazing photo shoot.

I'd also like to extend a huge "Thank You!" to all fans of my work and books—I created this beautiful journal for you.

Life is spectacular with you on my side!

What is your happiest vision?
Go there, stay there, and never leave!

DEDICATION

I dedicate this journal to all the brave dreamers and wishers!
You make the world magickal, and THAT we desperately need to keep
our heads up high and the sparkles glittering.

eautiful *manifester,*

THIS OUT-OF-THE-BLUE JOURNAL came to fruition because my inspirational son, a powerful manifester, once said:
"I'd give anything for..."
The aftermath you can probably guess.
Everything he would have given anything for happened for him just the way he spoke it, and this manifestation arrived with such speed (express delivery) that two weeks after, his whole life flipped completely changing him and his journey forever in the best way possible. But it didn't stop there; this magickal sentence shifted things big time for everyone involved and close to him too—also in terrific and somewhat unexpected ways.
So imagine me witnessing THAT happening, then trying it out for myself—with results showing it worked 100%.
Of course that made me wildly inspired to get this journal done ASAP since I am a lover of vividness and spontaneity.
But first I had to discuss this unexpected writing-detour with my partners in crime; my soul and the energetic part of me to ask if this new journal is in alignment with who I am, then I had a chat with the spirit of my business - FreakyHealer - to make sure it's in the cards time-wise and fits what I'm supposed to be doing; and lastly I checked with my spiritual guides who gave me the okay as long as it's not taking up too much time (get on it and do it quickly.) The universe took the stand of "this is unique and the world needs it," while consciousness guaranteed to deliver the words for me to channel with incredible speed. And with that, we had a deal!
"But why another manifestation journal?" you might ask.
Well, this is not just another manifestation tool in which you superficially come up with what you kinda sorta want, then leave everything up to the cosmos.

No, this book comes straight from the source and is your direct connection to your highest good. Think about it; you get to write about what you would give anything for, like your life depends on it, coming straight from your heart and delivered without any detours to the source—the most purest and brilliant force of energetic frequency there is and the only essence that can make anything happen for you.

The phrase "I'd give anything for…" carries a potent energy, one that has a fierceness and willingness attached to it—it's a strength and force like that of a mom protecting their children. It's a power, meaning you would fight for what you want and won't be denied. Think how you moving with such heroic energy can, and will, change your life—while manifesting what you want in such power.

Every new day you are asked to write down, "I'd give anything for…" your new day, but also for the bigger picture and future—your journaling will either have the same, different, or a mix of responses on any given day. At night you seal the day by writing about things that went great, showing gratitude for your day.

But there is more. Every day you are invited to read a quote and react to it in your own unique way, figuring out how you can apply this grandness into your every day.

Journaling through this manifestation book turns your wishes and dreams into reality—and we're talking express style (1. you express them, 2. they're delivered express-speed).

In such an equation you can experience life like you never have before, craft a time beyond your expectations, and love what you live—to the extent of becoming a pro in manifesting consciously and mindfully, feeling phenomenal while living the best of the best.

It's a change that is forever!

As a side note, there are a couple of bonus days at the end in case you ever find the need to do two in a day, or so you can keep working while your inspirational energy is flowing.

Enough chit-chat, I know you're ready—so grab your pen, and have incredible fun with catching more life than you have ever caught in your new manifesting ways.

                    Happiest,
                    Jacqueline

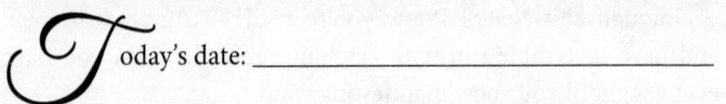 oday's date: _____

Start your sentence with: "I would give anything for…" and complete it with what you want and won't be denied for today. Be clear, write with an open heart, a smile, and ecstatic excitement.

_____
_____
_____
_____
_____

Start your sentence with: "I would give anything for…" and complete it with what you want and won't be denied for your far and near future—you know, the incredible big stuff you wish for.

_____
_____
_____
_____
_____

Time for night-night gratitude! Write down what went great today by starting your sentence with: "I am grateful for…" then add the good stuff and expect a night of sweet dreams.

_____
_____
_____
_____
_____

QUOTE

Free are those who know their value and carry themselves valued to their highest extent, anew and anew. - Jacqueline Pirtle

How can you carry yourself in such high value—how do you walk, talk, dress, and look in such worth? What's your facial expression, how do you feel, and how do you live your life in your highest value?

_____
_____
_____
_____
_____
_____
_____
_____
_____
_____
_____
_____

And so it is!

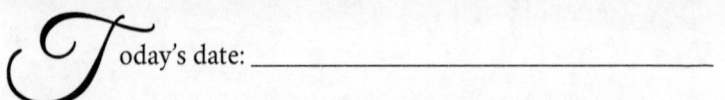
oday's date: _____

Start your sentence with: "I would give anything for..." and complete it with what you want and won't be denied for today. Be clear, write with an open heart, a smile, and ecstatic excitement.

_____
_____
_____
_____
_____

Start your sentence with: "I would give anything for..." and complete it with what you want and won't be denied for your far and near future—you know, the incredible big stuff you wish for.

_____
_____
_____
_____
_____

Time for night-night gratitude! Write down what went great today by starting your sentence with: "I am grateful for..." then add the good stuff and expect a night of sweet dreams.

_____
_____
_____
_____
_____

QUOTE

Yesterday was the past, but the memories stay for us to learn from. Today is the now and it's what you choose it to be. Tomorrow is your future, a never guaranteed entity. - Jacqueline Pirtle

How much do you live in the past? How much are you enjoying your now? How much do you live in the future? What can you do to live in a harmonious balance with all three existences?

_____
_____
_____
_____
_____
_____
_____
_____
_____
_____
_____
_____

And so it is!

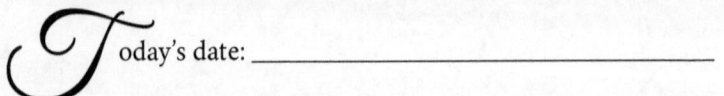
Today's date: _____

Start your sentence with: "I would give anything for..." and complete it with what you want and won't be denied for today. Be clear, write with an open heart, a smile, and ecstatic excitement.

_____
_____
_____
_____
_____

Start your sentence with: "I would give anything for..." and complete it with what you want and won't be denied for your far and near future—you know, the incredible big stuff you wish for.

_____
_____
_____
_____
_____

Time for night-night gratitude! Write down what went great today by starting your sentence with: "I am grateful for..." then add the good stuff and expect a night of sweet dreams.

_____
_____
_____
_____
_____

QUOTE

When in doubt, choose happiness! - Jacqueline Pirtle

What are your biggest doubts? How do they make you feel? How can you choose happiness above your doubts? What self-hint can you come up with so that when doubts arise, you know to shift into a happier place?

_____
_____
_____
_____
_____
_____
_____
_____
_____
_____
_____
_____
_____
_____

And so it is!

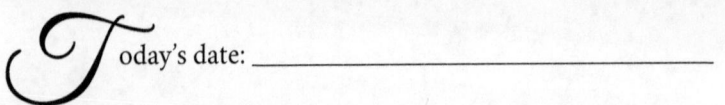Today's date: _____

START YOUR SENTENCE WITH: "I would give anything for..." and complete it with what you want and won't be denied for today. Be clear, write with an open heart, a smile, and ecstatic excitement.

_____
_____
_____
_____
_____

Start your sentence with: "I would give anything for..." and complete it with what you want and won't be denied for your far and near future—you know, the incredible big stuff you wish for.

_____
_____
_____
_____
_____

Time for night-night gratitude! Write down what went great today by starting your sentence with: "I am grateful for..." then add the good stuff and expect a night of sweet dreams.

_____
_____
_____
_____
_____

QUOTE

Abundance is everywhere—around you, in you, and as you.
- Jacqueline Pirtle

What is abundance for you? How does it feel? Where, when, and how do you experience abundance? How can you focus on all abundance, that's naturally everywhere, when scarcity hits the fan?

_____
_____
_____
_____
_____
_____
_____
_____
_____
_____
_____
_____

And so it is!

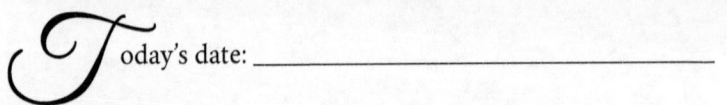oday's date: _____

START YOUR SENTENCE WITH: "I would give anything for..." and complete it with what you want and won't be denied for today. Be clear, write with an open heart, a smile, and ecstatic excitement.

_____
_____
_____
_____
_____

Start your sentence with: "I would give anything for..." and complete it with what you want and won't be denied for your far and near future—you know, the incredible big stuff you wish for.

_____
_____
_____
_____
_____

Time for night-night gratitude! Write down what went great today by starting your sentence with: "I am grateful for..." then add the good stuff and expect a night of sweet dreams.

_____
_____
_____
_____
_____

QUOTE

Feeling good is easy to like, while feeling bad - angry, hopeless, sad, lost, in grief, misunderstood, deceived and such - is hard to fit in the "I like it" box. - Jacqueline Pirtle

Why is it easy to like feeling good? What is hard to accept when you feel bad? How can you embrace feeling bad as a normal part of you—or even better, how can you start celebrating your bad feelings for what they are; gifts in disguise, since they hold the deep wisdom of your truth?

_____
_____
_____
_____
_____
_____
_____
_____
_____

And so it is!

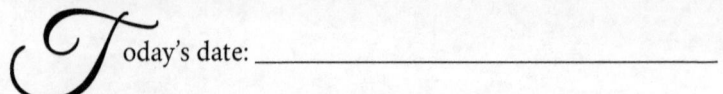

Today's date: _____

START YOUR SENTENCE WITH: "I would give anything for..." and complete it with what you want and won't be denied for today. Be clear, write with an open heart, a smile, and ecstatic excitement.

_____
_____
_____
_____
_____

Start your sentence with: "I would give anything for..." and complete it with what you want and won't be denied for your far and near future—you know, the incredible big stuff you wish for.

_____
_____
_____
_____
_____

Time for night-night gratitude! Write down what went great today by starting your sentence with: "I am grateful for..." then add the good stuff and expect a night of sweet dreams.

_____
_____
_____
_____
_____

QUOTE

Weather is a strength barometer, showing how rooted or frail your determination to be happy is. - Jacqueline Pirtle

How does the weather affect you? What is your go-to weather for instant happiness? How can you shift your bad-weather mood to feeling great anyways—could you learn to enjoy what you call "bad" weather outside? Come up with an "I am happy anyways" weather plan!

_____
_____
_____
_____
_____
_____
_____
_____
_____
_____
_____

And so it is!

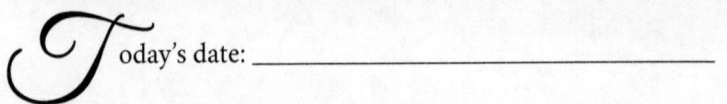

oday's date: _____

START YOUR SENTENCE WITH: "I would give anything for…" and complete it with what you want and won't be denied for today. Be clear, write with an open heart, a smile, and ecstatic excitement.

_____
_____
_____
_____
_____

Start your sentence with: "I would give anything for…" and complete it with what you want and won't be denied for your far and near future—you know, the incredible big stuff you wish for.

_____
_____
_____
_____
_____

Time for night-night gratitude! Write down what went great today by starting your sentence with: "I am grateful for…" then add the good stuff and expect a night of sweet dreams.

_____
_____
_____
_____
_____

QUOTE

Food is a tool for happiness, health, abundance, and success.
- Jacqueline Pirtle

What part does food play in your allover well-being? Do you have favorites in a certain category? Why is that so? What do you like about these foods, and how do they make you feel? Could you feel that great with non-food things too—find equals that lift you up like that? One more tricky question: could you choose better foods to feel happier, healthier, more abundant, and super successful?

_____
_____
_____
_____
_____
_____
_____
_____

And so it is!

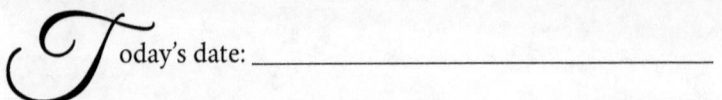 oday's date: _____

Start your sentence with: "I would give anything for…" and complete it with what you want and won't be denied for today. Be clear, write with an open heart, a smile, and ecstatic excitement.

_____
_____
_____
_____
_____

Start your sentence with: "I would give anything for…" and complete it with what you want and won't be denied for your far and near future—you know, the incredible big stuff you wish for.

_____
_____
_____
_____
_____

Time for night-night gratitude! Write down what went great today by starting your sentence with: "I am grateful for…" then add the good stuff and expect a night of sweet dreams.

_____
_____
_____
_____
_____

QUOTE

Crying equates strength because it tells how strongly you care, how powerful your emotions are, and how maturely you cleanse your body, mind, and soul with these tears. - Jacqueline Pirtle

Do you like to cry? How many times do you cry? How do you feel when you cry or have cried? Do you judge yourself when you cry —or do others judge you when your tears are falling? Are you aware that only strong people cry, since it takes guts to care - or feel - so deeply that you can cry?

_____
_____
_____
_____
_____
_____
_____
_____
_____

And so it is!

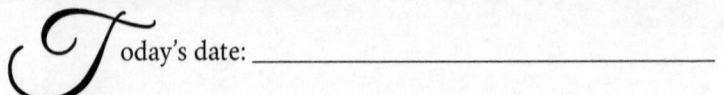 oday's date: _____

START YOUR SENTENCE WITH: "I would give anything for…" and complete it with what you want and won't be denied for today. Be clear, write with an open heart, a smile, and ecstatic excitement.

_____
_____
_____
_____
_____

Start your sentence with: "I would give anything for…" and complete it with what you want and won't be denied for your far and near future—you know, the incredible big stuff you wish for.

_____
_____
_____
_____
_____

Time for night-night gratitude! Write down what went great today by starting your sentence with: "I am grateful for…" then add the good stuff and expect a night of sweet dreams.

_____
_____
_____
_____
_____

QUOTE

Your weaknesses show you the way to your goodnesses.
- Jacqueline Pirtle

How do you feel about the word weak? Do you know your weaknesses? How do you feel about them? Can you embrace where and when you feel weak, then focus on building strength there—initiating your goodnesses big time?

_____
_____
_____
_____
_____
_____
_____
_____
_____
_____
_____
_____

And so it is!

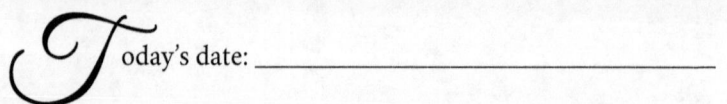

Today's date: _____

Start your sentence with: "I would give anything for..." and complete it with what you want and won't be denied for today. Be clear, write with an open heart, a smile, and ecstatic excitement.

_____
_____
_____
_____
_____

Start your sentence with: "I would give anything for..." and complete it with what you want and won't be denied for your far and near future—you know, the incredible big stuff you wish for.

_____
_____
_____
_____
_____

Time for night-night gratitude! Write down what went great today by starting your sentence with: "I am grateful for..." then add the good stuff and expect a night of sweet dreams.

_____
_____
_____
_____
_____

QUOTE

Happiness is a string made of little bliss and joy pockets. How long that string is depends on you. - Jacqueline Pirtle

How long is your happy string? How often do you crate joy bubbles to keep your string going? How can you get more determined to prioritize creating little bliss moments here and there?

_____
_____
_____
_____
_____
_____
_____
_____
_____
_____
_____
_____
_____

And so it is!

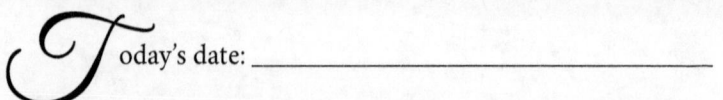 oday's date: _____

Start your sentence with: "I would give anything for…" and complete it with what you want and won't be denied for today. Be clear, write with an open heart, a smile, and ecstatic excitement.

_____
_____
_____
_____
_____

Start your sentence with: "I would give anything for…" and complete it with what you want and won't be denied for your far and near future—you know, the incredible big stuff you wish for.

_____
_____
_____
_____
_____

Time for night-night gratitude! Write down what went great today by starting your sentence with: "I am grateful for…" then add the good stuff and expect a night of sweet dreams.

_____
_____
_____
_____
_____

QUOTE

Humor and success are your friends for a lifetime—they love to hang out and enjoy digging into your whole essence because that's what best friends are for. - Jacqueline Pirtle

What does this quote spark for you? Are you feeling this friendship with excitement? How deep are humor and success entrenched into your life, and how solid is your kinship with these two? Do you think your humor and success goes hand in hand?

_____
_____
_____
_____
_____
_____
_____
_____
_____
_____

And so it is!

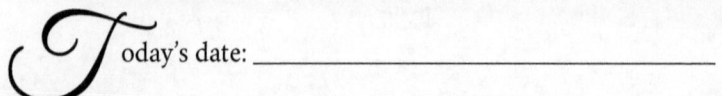

Today's date: _____

START YOUR SENTENCE WITH: "I would give anything for…" and complete it with what you want and won't be denied for today. Be clear, write with an open heart, a smile, and ecstatic excitement.

_____
_____
_____
_____
_____

Start your sentence with: "I would give anything for…" and complete it with what you want and won't be denied for your far and near future—you know, the incredible big stuff you wish for.

_____
_____
_____
_____
_____

Time for night-night gratitude! Write down what went great today by starting your sentence with: "I am grateful for…" then add the good stuff and expect a night of sweet dreams.

_____
_____
_____
_____
_____

QUOTE

Realizing who you are, newly, in every split second means you walk in your aligned power at all times. - Jacqueline Pirtle

Did you know that you are always new—but also that life is always new? How can you live your life differently knowing, or being reminded, that everything always is new and filled with new choices and possibilities?

_____
_____
_____
_____
_____
_____
_____
_____
_____
_____
_____
_____

And so it is!

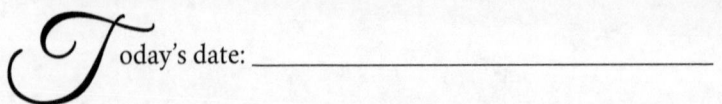oday's date: _____

START YOUR SENTENCE WITH: "I would give anything for…" and complete it with what you want and won't be denied for today. Be clear, write with an open heart, a smile, and ecstatic excitement.

_____
_____
_____
_____
_____

Start your sentence with: "I would give anything for…" and complete it with what you want and won't be denied for your far and near future—you know, the incredible big stuff you wish for.

_____
_____
_____
_____
_____

Time for night-night gratitude! Write down what went great today by starting your sentence with: "I am grateful for…" then add the good stuff and expect a night of sweet dreams.

_____
_____
_____
_____
_____

QUOTE

Reaching for your phone means you're not reaching for a loved one.
- Jacqueline Pirtle

How many times a day are you picking up your phone? Could you stop yourself and reach for your loves instead? What would that do not only for you, but also for others and your relationships with them?

_____
_____
_____
_____
_____
_____
_____
_____
_____
_____
_____
_____

And so it is!

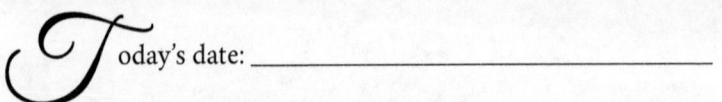oday's date: _____

Start your sentence with: "I would give anything for…" and complete it with what you want and won't be denied for today. Be clear, write with an open heart, a smile, and ecstatic excitement.

_____
_____
_____
_____
_____

Start your sentence with: "I would give anything for…" and complete it with what you want and won't be denied for your far and near future—you know, the incredible big stuff you wish for.

_____
_____
_____
_____
_____

Time for night-night gratitude! Write down what went great today by starting your sentence with: "I am grateful for…" then add the good stuff and expect a night of sweet dreams.

_____
_____
_____
_____
_____

QUOTE

Being a good human being is very unique to each and every one of us.
- Jacqueline Pirtle

What does "being a good human being" mean to you? How can you be a better version of your unique good? How can you inspire others to be grander too?

_____
_____
_____
_____
_____
_____
_____
_____
_____
_____
_____
_____

And so it is!

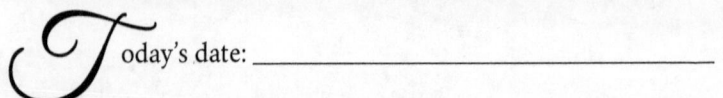
Today's date: _____

Start your sentence with: "I would give anything for…" and complete it with what you want and won't be denied for today. Be clear, write with an open heart, a smile, and ecstatic excitement.

_____
_____
_____
_____
_____

Start your sentence with: "I would give anything for…" and complete it with what you want and won't be denied for your far and near future—you know, the incredible big stuff you wish for.

_____
_____
_____
_____
_____

Time for night-night gratitude! Write down what went great today by starting your sentence with: "I am grateful for…" then add the good stuff and expect a night of sweet dreams.

_____
_____
_____
_____
_____

QUOTE

The big picture asks you to try to understand more deeply while the little picture invites you to experience life more mindfully.
- Jacqueline Pirtle

What is the big picture in your personal life, but also in your world view? How does the little picture look for you—and for the world? How can you combine the learning with the experiencing?

_____
_____
_____
_____
_____
_____
_____
_____
_____
_____
_____

And so it is!

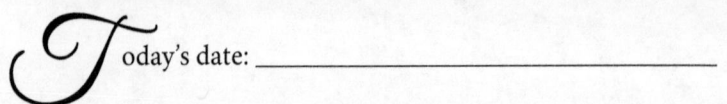 Today's date: _____

Start your sentence with: "I would give anything for…" and complete it with what you want and won't be denied for today. Be clear, write with an open heart, a smile, and ecstatic excitement.

_____
_____
_____
_____
_____

Start your sentence with: "I would give anything for…" and complete it with what you want and won't be denied for your far and near future—you know, the incredible big stuff you wish for.

_____
_____
_____
_____
_____

Time for night-night gratitude! Write down what went great today by starting your sentence with: "I am grateful for…" then add the good stuff and expect a night of sweet dreams.

_____
_____
_____
_____
_____

QUOTE

Hope blasts downer-feelings away by lifting those who hope into the sky —leaving the downer feelings where they belong; down below.
- Jacqueline Pirtle

What is hope for you and how does it feel? How can you create more of the hope-emotions—what can you reach for to initiate feelings of hope? In contrast, how do the downer-feelings make you feel—do you see any patterns of yours that are creating your downward spiral? Take these insights as a baseline and any time you feel less than hope, shift higher into your hope-ways, leaving the downs behind.

_____
_____
_____
_____
_____
_____
_____

And so it is!

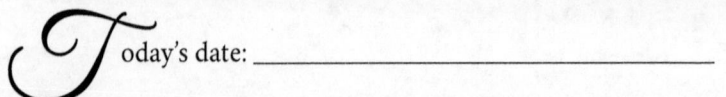 oday's date: _____

START YOUR SENTENCE WITH: "I would give anything for…" and complete it with what you want and won't be denied for today. Be clear, write with an open heart, a smile, and ecstatic excitement.

_____
_____
_____
_____
_____

Start your sentence with: "I would give anything for…" and complete it with what you want and won't be denied for your far and near future—you know, the incredible big stuff you wish for.

_____
_____
_____
_____
_____

Time for night-night gratitude! Write down what went great today by starting your sentence with: "I am grateful for…" then add the good stuff and expect a night of sweet dreams.

_____
_____
_____
_____
_____

QUOTE

Letting go and leaving everything behind is a new start—a rebirth.
- Jacqueline Pirtle

How can you give birth to a new you, one that is fitting for you now and today? What can you let go of? What does your new you look like—how are you moving, speaking, thinking, behaving? What is your new smile like? How does it feel to laugh in new ways?

_____
_____
_____
_____
_____
_____
_____
_____
_____
_____
_____

And so it is!

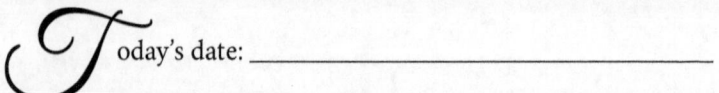oday's date: _____

START YOUR SENTENCE WITH: "I would give anything for…" and complete it with what you want and won't be denied for today. Be clear, write with an open heart, a smile, and ecstatic excitement.

_____
_____
_____
_____
_____

Start your sentence with: "I would give anything for…" and complete it with what you want and won't be denied for your far and near future—you know, the incredible big stuff you wish for.

_____
_____
_____
_____
_____

Time for night-night gratitude! Write down what went great today by starting your sentence with: "I am grateful for…" then add the good stuff and expect a night of sweet dreams.

_____
_____
_____
_____
_____

QUOTE

Removing yourself from the non-fitting is power. - Jacqueline Pirtle

How can you remove yourself when it's not your vibe? How will you know that it's not your vibe? Clarity wins here, because there's no need to stay put in what does not feel good.

___
___
___
___
___
___
___
___
___
___
___
___
___
___

And so it is!

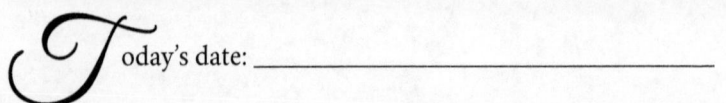oday's date: _____

Start your sentence with: "I would give anything for..." and complete it with what you want and won't be denied for today. Be clear, write with an open heart, a smile, and ecstatic excitement.

_____
_____
_____
_____
_____

Start your sentence with: "I would give anything for..." and complete it with what you want and won't be denied for your far and near future—you know, the incredible big stuff you wish for.

_____
_____
_____
_____
_____

Time for night-night gratitude! Write down what went great today by starting your sentence with: "I am grateful for..." then add the good stuff and expect a night of sweet dreams.

_____
_____
_____
_____
_____

QUOTE

Satisfied beings walk with an open heart, because their satisfaction serves like a shield that's saying "Can't mess with my bliss!"
- Jacqueline Pirtle

How does satisfaction feel for you? What gives you the most satisfaction ever? How can you create even more satisfaction for yourself and loved ones? Can you visualize your satisfaction-shield to imprint it into your mind, body, and soul?

_____
_____
_____
_____
_____
_____
_____
_____
_____
_____

And so it is!

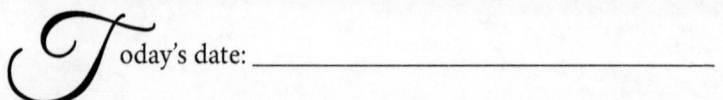oday's date: _____

START YOUR SENTENCE WITH: "I would give anything for…" and complete it with what you want and won't be denied for today. Be clear, write with an open heart, a smile, and ecstatic excitement.

_____
_____
_____
_____
_____

Start your sentence with: "I would give anything for…" and complete it with what you want and won't be denied for your far and near future—you know, the incredible big stuff you wish for.

_____
_____
_____
_____
_____

Time for night-night gratitude! Write down what went great today by starting your sentence with: "I am grateful for…" then add the good stuff and expect a night of sweet dreams.

_____
_____
_____
_____
_____

QUOTE

Love acts like a bridge for consciousness to cross into physical life, showing that life and the world is truly beautiful. - Jacqueline Pirtle

Do you see the beauty in life? Where do you witness it mostly? How can you focus more on all the gorgeousness and well-being right in front of you? How can you share your big love openly and freely—acting as a connector between consciousness and the physical?

_____
_____
_____
_____
_____
_____
_____
_____
_____
_____

And so it is!

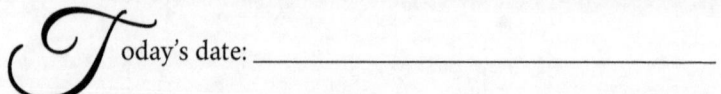

Today's date: _____

Start your sentence with: "I would give anything for..." and complete it with what you want and won't be denied for today. Be clear, write with an open heart, a smile, and ecstatic excitement.

_____
_____
_____
_____
_____

Start your sentence with: "I would give anything for..." and complete it with what you want and won't be denied for your far and near future—you know, the incredible big stuff you wish for.

_____
_____
_____
_____
_____

Time for night-night gratitude! Write down what went great today by starting your sentence with: "I am grateful for..." then add the good stuff and expect a night of sweet dreams.

_____
_____
_____
_____
_____

QUOTE

Most problems are best solved with a smile, some forgiveness, and relaxation. - Jacqueline Pirtle

Are you willing to try to solve your issues like that? How can you stay calm and remember to do so when heated or stressed? Report back here about your successes—but also where and when this did not work and why. Learn from you!

_____
_____
_____
_____
_____
_____
_____
_____
_____
_____
_____
_____

And so it is!

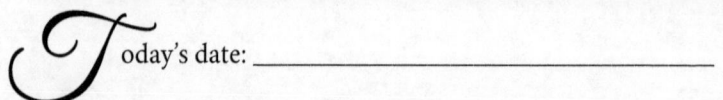

Today's date: _____

Start your sentence with: "I would give anything for…" and complete it with what you want and won't be denied for today. Be clear, write with an open heart, a smile, and ecstatic excitement.

_____
_____
_____
_____
_____

Start your sentence with: "I would give anything for…" and complete it with what you want and won't be denied for your far and near future—you know, the incredible big stuff you wish for.

_____
_____
_____
_____
_____

Time for night-night gratitude! Write down what went great today by starting your sentence with: "I am grateful for…" then add the good stuff and expect a night of sweet dreams.

_____
_____
_____
_____
_____

QUOTE

Wings are for angels and you, my beautiful manifester, definitely have wings. - Jacqueline Pirtle

What is your angelic side—how does it feel? How do your wings look, feel, and what are they there for? How did you use your wings in the past, or how did you not? How can you use them now that you are truly aware of them? What superpowers do your wings have—besides giving you the freedom of flight?

_____
_____
_____
_____
_____
_____
_____
_____
_____
_____
_____

And so it is!

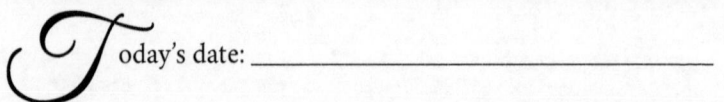oday's date: _____

START YOUR SENTENCE WITH: "I would give anything for…" and complete it with what you want and won't be denied for today. Be clear, write with an open heart, a smile, and ecstatic excitement.

_____
_____
_____
_____
_____

Start your sentence with: "I would give anything for…" and complete it with what you want and won't be denied for your far and near future—you know, the incredible big stuff you wish for.

_____
_____
_____
_____
_____

Time for night-night gratitude! Write down what went great today by starting your sentence with: "I am grateful for…" then add the good stuff and expect a night of sweet dreams.

_____
_____
_____
_____
_____

QUOTE

Anger is nothing else than energy, and a powerful focus of it indeed.
- Jacqueline Pirtle

How is your relationship with anger? Do you love it or hate it? Do you embrace it or judge yourself when angry? What makes you angry the most—and how could you shift your anger into a higher feeling energy, like compassion, acceptance, or even love? Knowing that anger is a powerful energy, what could you use that force for when it arises; cleaning the house, mowing the grass, exercise?

_____
_____
_____
_____
_____
_____
_____
_____

And so it is!

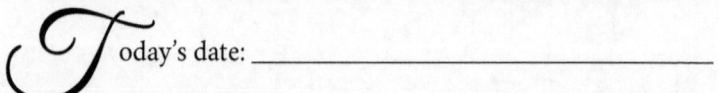Today's date: _____

Start your sentence with: "I would give anything for…" and complete it with what you want and won't be denied for today. Be clear, write with an open heart, a smile, and ecstatic excitement.

_____
_____
_____
_____
_____

Start your sentence with: "I would give anything for…" and complete it with what you want and won't be denied for your far and near future—you know, the incredible big stuff you wish for.

_____
_____
_____
_____
_____

Time for night-night gratitude! Write down what went great today by starting your sentence with: "I am grateful for…" then add the good stuff and expect a night of sweet dreams.

_____
_____
_____
_____
_____

QUOTE

Feeling over the moon has many facets. - Jacqueline Pirtle

When do you feel like you could hug the world? How many different "over the moon" dimensions do you know of and what are the specifics of these feelings, situations, and moments? How can you create even more times of bliss?

_____
_____
_____
_____
_____
_____
_____
_____
_____
_____
_____
_____
_____

And so it is!

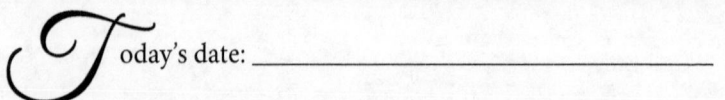
Today's date: _____

Start your sentence with: "I would give anything for…" and complete it with what you want and won't be denied for today. Be clear, write with an open heart, a smile, and ecstatic excitement.

_____
_____
_____
_____
_____

Start your sentence with: "I would give anything for…" and complete it with what you want and won't be denied for your far and near future—you know, the incredible big stuff you wish for.

_____
_____
_____
_____
_____

Time for night-night gratitude! Write down what went great today by starting your sentence with: "I am grateful for…" then add the good stuff and expect a night of sweet dreams.

_____
_____
_____
_____
_____

QUOTE

Existing wholesomely as the true you is the foundation of a healthy, happy, abundant, and successful life. - Jacqueline Pirtle

What does "existing" as you mean to you? Do you exist fully as you: physically, mentally, emotionally, energetically, and spiritually? Or how much are you existing partially—and how can you step into complete existence? Since you are an ever-changing being, how can you keep up with existing newly anew and anew?

_____
_____
_____
_____
_____
_____
_____
_____
_____
_____
_____

And so it is!

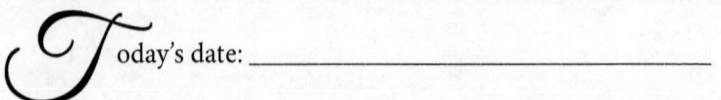

Today's date: _____

Start your sentence with: "I would give anything for…" and complete it with what you want and won't be denied for today. Be clear, write with an open heart, a smile, and ecstatic excitement.

_____
_____
_____
_____
_____

Start your sentence with: "I would give anything for…" and complete it with what you want and won't be denied for your far and near future—you know, the incredible big stuff you wish for.

_____
_____
_____
_____
_____

Time for night-night gratitude! Write down what went great today by starting your sentence with: "I am grateful for…" then add the good stuff and expect a night of sweet dreams.

_____
_____
_____
_____
_____

QUOTE

Sleep, baby, sleep—because that's when dreams form lives and miracles become real. - Jacqueline Pirtle

Do you like sleep? If yes, how does it feel to sleep? If not, why is it that you don't enjoy that sleepy siesta—and how could you change that? Do you remember your dreams? If yes, what are they? If no, could you take a mindful moment when waking up and sense what you dreamt about? Lastly, how do you feel about miracles? What miracles are you wishing for, and how can you live like your miracles are already present? What would it take for you to focus on the miracles in your new day?

_____
_____
_____
_____
_____
_____
_____

And so it is!

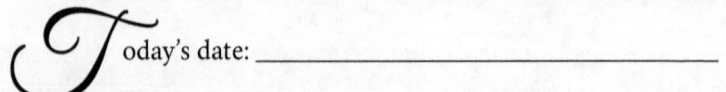 oday's date: _____

Start your sentence with: "I would give anything for..." and complete it with what you want and won't be denied for today. Be clear, write with an open heart, a smile, and ecstatic excitement.

_____
_____
_____
_____
_____

Start your sentence with: "I would give anything for..." and complete it with what you want and won't be denied for your far and near future—you know, the incredible big stuff you wish for.

_____
_____
_____
_____
_____

Time for night-night gratitude! Write down what went great today by starting your sentence with: "I am grateful for..." then add the good stuff and expect a night of sweet dreams.

_____
_____
_____
_____
_____

QUOTE

Singing and dancing frees the mind, body, and soul. - Jacqueline Pirtle

What do you think would happen, if you sang and danced often? How much freer would your physical body, mind, emotions, and your energetic you be and feel? How can you incorporate more singing and dancing into your days? Who would you like to sing and dance with—inspiring them to be free too?

_____
_____
_____
_____
_____
_____
_____
_____
_____
_____
_____
_____
_____

And so it is!

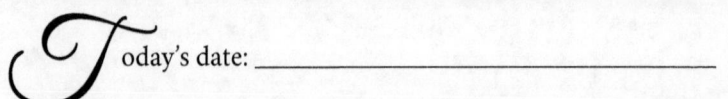 oday's date: _____

Start your sentence with: "I would give anything for…" and complete it with what you want and won't be denied for today. Be clear, write with an open heart, a smile, and ecstatic excitement.

_____
_____
_____
_____
_____

Start your sentence with: "I would give anything for…" and complete it with what you want and won't be denied for your far and near future—you know, the incredible big stuff you wish for.

_____
_____
_____
_____
_____

Time for night-night gratitude! Write down what went great today by starting your sentence with: "I am grateful for…" then add the good stuff and expect a night of sweet dreams.

_____
_____
_____
_____
_____

QUOTE

Not every thought has to be spoken aloud. - Jacqueline Pirtle

What are the thoughts you speak, but feel they should not be spoken? Why did you say them anyway? How can you control yourself to know and feel when to stop talking, realizing that this halt is better for you? Could you journal them instead?

_____
_____
_____
_____
_____
_____
_____
_____
_____
_____
_____
_____

And so it is!

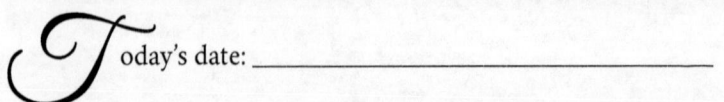oday's date: _____

Start your sentence with: "I would give anything for…" and complete it with what you want and won't be denied for today. Be clear, write with an open heart, a smile, and ecstatic excitement.

_____
_____
_____
_____
_____

Start your sentence with: "I would give anything for…" and complete it with what you want and won't be denied for your far and near future—you know, the incredible big stuff you wish for.

_____
_____
_____
_____
_____

Time for night-night gratitude! Write down what went great today by starting your sentence with: "I am grateful for…" then add the good stuff and expect a night of sweet dreams.

_____
_____
_____
_____
_____

QUOTE

"I let life be life!" - Jacqueline Pirtle

Speak these words, and maybe even shrug your shoulders too! Do you feel the ease in this? How can you use this effortlessness in your new days ahead, in your life, especially when things are tough? How can you share this tip with others who could use this easiness too?

_____
_____
_____
_____
_____
_____
_____
_____
_____
_____
_____
_____

And so it is!

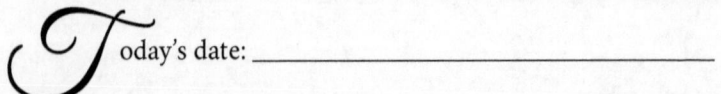oday's date: _____

START YOUR SENTENCE WITH: "I would give anything for…" and complete it with what you want and won't be denied for today. Be clear, write with an open heart, a smile, and ecstatic excitement.

_____
_____
_____
_____
_____

Start your sentence with: "I would give anything for…" and complete it with what you want and won't be denied for your far and near future—you know, the incredible big stuff you wish for.

_____
_____
_____
_____
_____

Time for night-night gratitude! Write down what went great today by starting your sentence with: "I am grateful for…" then add the good stuff and expect a night of sweet dreams.

_____
_____
_____
_____
_____

QUOTE

Anything material is a tool in physical life, while everything energetic is the foundation of all. - Jacqueline Pirtle

What material things do you love in life? Don't judge yourself, materialism is here to enjoy. How do you use these tools to be happy—how do they make you feel? What does it mean to you; "Energy is the foundation of all"? How does that all tie in for you?

_____
_____
_____
_____
_____
_____
_____
_____
_____
_____
_____
_____

And so it is!

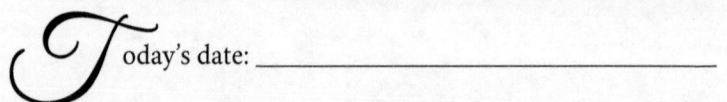oday's date: _____

START YOUR SENTENCE WITH: "I would give anything for…" and complete it with what you want and won't be denied for today. Be clear, write with an open heart, a smile, and ecstatic excitement.

_____
_____
_____
_____
_____

Start your sentence with: "I would give anything for…" and complete it with what you want and won't be denied for your far and near future—you know, the incredible big stuff you wish for.

_____
_____
_____
_____
_____

Time for night-night gratitude! Write down what went great today by starting your sentence with: "I am grateful for…" then add the good stuff and expect a night of sweet dreams.

_____
_____
_____
_____
_____

QUOTE

Character and personality is key. - Jacqueline Pirtle

What is your character—your core beliefs, personal, moral, and ethical quality? What is your personality—"you" from top to bottom; all the behaviors, interests, thoughts, beliefs, experiences, and traits that make you unique in the world?

_____
_____
_____
_____
_____
_____
_____
_____
_____
_____
_____
_____
_____

And so it is!

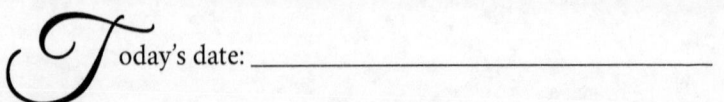Today's date: _____

START YOUR SENTENCE WITH: "I would give anything for..." and complete it with what you want and won't be denied for today. Be clear, write with an open heart, a smile, and ecstatic excitement.

_____
_____
_____
_____
_____

Start your sentence with: "I would give anything for..." and complete it with what you want and won't be denied for your far and near future—you know, the incredible big stuff you wish for.

_____
_____
_____
_____
_____

Time for night-night gratitude! Write down what went great today by starting your sentence with: "I am grateful for..." then add the good stuff and expect a night of sweet dreams.

_____
_____
_____
_____
_____

QUOTE

Adventure is the oxygen of life. - Jacqueline Pirtle

How are you in the adventure compartment? Do you like to explore freely? What is your favorite, most wild and exciting, undertaking? How do you feel on these quests? What small and big ones could you add—to oxygenize the essence of your life?

_____
_____
_____
_____
_____
_____
_____
_____
_____
_____
_____
_____
_____

And so it is!

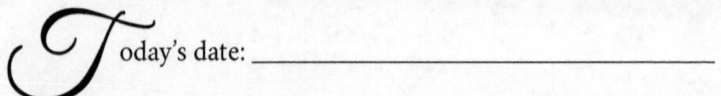

Today's date: _____

START YOUR SENTENCE WITH: "I would give anything for..." and complete it with what you want and won't be denied for today. Be clear, write with an open heart, a smile, and ecstatic excitement.

_____
_____
_____
_____
_____

Start your sentence with: "I would give anything for..." and complete it with what you want and won't be denied for your far and near future—you know, the incredible big stuff you wish for.

_____
_____
_____
_____
_____

Time for night-night gratitude! Write down what went great today by starting your sentence with: "I am grateful for..." then add the good stuff and expect a night of sweet dreams.

_____
_____
_____
_____
_____

QUOTE

Everything in life is always a choice, so choose wisely and choose newly often—but also own your choices. - Jacqueline Pirtle

What in your life is not working—what "new" could you choose to make it work? How can you incorporate pauses into your day—to choose wiser, more mindfully, and aligned? What steps can you take to own all your choices, even the ones that feel wrong? And how could you refrain from making others responsible for your choices, to stop giving away your power?

_____
_____
_____
_____
_____
_____
_____
_____
_____
_____

And so it is!

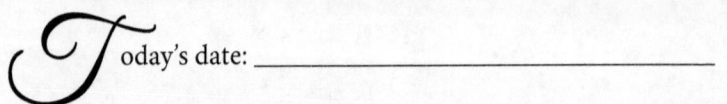

Today's date: _____

Start your sentence with: "I would give anything for..." and complete it with what you want and won't be denied for today. Be clear, write with an open heart, a smile, and ecstatic excitement.

_____
_____
_____
_____
_____

Start your sentence with: "I would give anything for..." and complete it with what you want and won't be denied for your far and near future—you know, the incredible big stuff you wish for.

_____
_____
_____
_____
_____

Time for night-night gratitude! Write down what went great today by starting your sentence with: "I am grateful for..." then add the good stuff and expect a night of sweet dreams.

_____
_____
_____
_____
_____

QUOTE

Wonder away, because in that state of curiosity unlimited possibilities are a given—leading to the fact that everything is possible.
- Jacqueline Pirtle

How can you practice being in wonder in your day-to-day life? What do you think will happen, making this wonder-feeling your normal state of living and being?

_____
_____
_____
_____
_____
_____
_____
_____
_____
_____
_____
_____

And so it is!

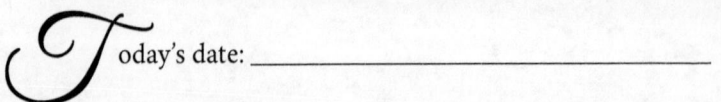oday's date: _____

Start your sentence with: "I would give anything for..." and complete it with what you want and won't be denied for today. Be clear, write with an open heart, a smile, and ecstatic excitement.

_____
_____
_____
_____
_____

Start your sentence with: "I would give anything for..." and complete it with what you want and won't be denied for your far and near future—you know, the incredible big stuff you wish for.

_____
_____
_____
_____
_____

Time for night-night gratitude! Write down what went great today by starting your sentence with: "I am grateful for..." then add the good stuff and expect a night of sweet dreams.

_____
_____
_____
_____
_____

QUOTE

Rainy days scream for colors! - Jacqueline Pirtle

Do you like colors? Which are your favorite, and how do they make you feel? Now visualize a rainy day with grey skies. What would happen if your favorite colors would paint that sky? Does your mood and all over well-being change? How? Why?

_____
_____
_____
_____
_____
_____
_____
_____
_____
_____
_____
_____
_____

And so it is!

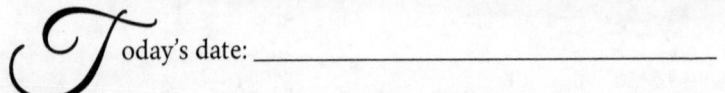oday's date: _____

START YOUR SENTENCE WITH: "I would give anything for..." and complete it with what you want and won't be denied for today. Be clear, write with an open heart, a smile, and ecstatic excitement.

_____
_____
_____
_____
_____

Start your sentence with: "I would give anything for..." and complete it with what you want and won't be denied for your far and near future—you know, the incredible big stuff you wish for.

_____
_____
_____
_____
_____

Time for night-night gratitude! Write down what went great today by starting your sentence with: "I am grateful for..." then add the good stuff and expect a night of sweet dreams.

_____
_____
_____
_____
_____

QUOTE

Simplicity wins—just think how a simple "Thank you" can change everything. - Jacqueline Pirtle

What is simplicity to you? Can you come up with simple words and actions that would change your life, or someone else's? How can you plan your future on a foundation of simplicity?

_____
_____
_____
_____
_____
_____
_____
_____
_____
_____
_____
_____
_____

And so it is!

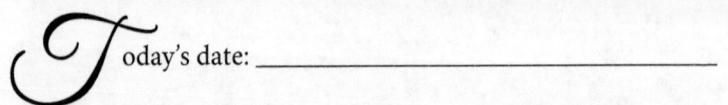
Today's date: _____

Start your sentence with: "I would give anything for…" and complete it with what you want and won't be denied for today. Be clear, write with an open heart, a smile, and ecstatic excitement.

_____
_____
_____
_____
_____

Start your sentence with: "I would give anything for…" and complete it with what you want and won't be denied for your far and near future—you know, the incredible big stuff you wish for.

_____
_____
_____
_____
_____

Time for night-night gratitude! Write down what went great today by starting your sentence with: "I am grateful for…" then add the good stuff and expect a night of sweet dreams.

_____
_____
_____
_____
_____

QUOTE

Letting go is guaranteeing your inner peace. - Jacqueline Pirtle

What are you holding onto that creates havoc inside of you? Why are you treasuring such darkness like it's worth gold—when in truth it's nothing but gunk? How can you step over to the peaceful side where letting it all go is the norm?

_____
_____
_____
_____
_____
_____
_____
_____
_____
_____
_____
_____
_____
_____

And so it is!

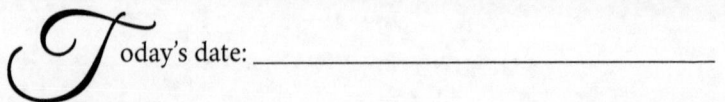Today's date: _____

Start your sentence with: "I would give anything for…" and complete it with what you want and won't be denied for today. Be clear, write with an open heart, a smile, and ecstatic excitement.

_____
_____
_____
_____
_____

Start your sentence with: "I would give anything for…" and complete it with what you want and won't be denied for your far and near future—you know, the incredible big stuff you wish for.

_____
_____
_____
_____
_____

Time for night-night gratitude! Write down what went great today by starting your sentence with: "I am grateful for…" then add the good stuff and expect a night of sweet dreams.

_____
_____
_____
_____
_____

QUOTE

It's never that bad! - Jacqueline Pirtle

What does this saying make you feel at first? Now close your eyes and breathe deeply 5 times—how do you feel about these words now? See how you are wired for a naysayer reaction towards this quote, but that after aligning with inner peace you see, feel, and think about things differently—entertaining the thought that it's actually never that bad? How can you apply the aligned meaning of this quote to your everyday, and live relaxed even when things are tough?

_____
_____
_____
_____
_____
_____
_____
_____
_____

And so it is!

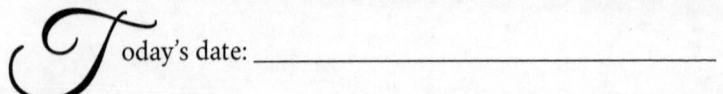

Today's date: _____

Start your sentence with: "I would give anything for..." and complete it with what you want and won't be denied for today. Be clear, write with an open heart, a smile, and ecstatic excitement.

_____
_____
_____
_____
_____

Start your sentence with: "I would give anything for..." and complete it with what you want and won't be denied for your far and near future—you know, the incredible big stuff you wish for.

_____
_____
_____
_____
_____

Time for night-night gratitude! Write down what went great today by starting your sentence with: "I am grateful for..." then add the good stuff and expect a night of sweet dreams.

_____
_____
_____
_____
_____

QUOTE

To fly, you need wings! - Jacqueline Pirtle

How healthy are your wings? Use your creative imagination here. How can you nurture your wings to fly even higher and free? Where do your wings take you? What immobilizes your wings in life?

_____
_____
_____
_____
_____
_____
_____
_____
_____
_____
_____
_____

And so it is!

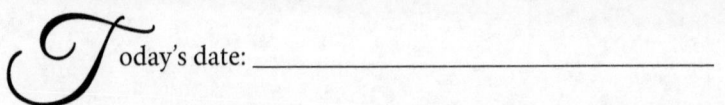Today's date: _____

Start your sentence with: "I would give anything for..." and complete it with what you want and won't be denied for today. Be clear, write with an open heart, a smile, and ecstatic excitement.

_____
_____
_____
_____
_____

Start your sentence with: "I would give anything for..." and complete it with what you want and won't be denied for your far and near future—you know, the incredible big stuff you wish for.

_____
_____
_____
_____
_____

Time for night-night gratitude! Write down what went great today by starting your sentence with: "I am grateful for..." then add the good stuff and expect a night of sweet dreams.

_____
_____
_____
_____
_____

QUOTE

You are never stuck, just not aligned. - Jacqueline Pirtle

How does it feel when you think that you are stuck? Where in life do you feel like you are stuck? Knowing that "stuck" is being unaligned with who you are, how does it feel being unaligned—why are you unaligned? What tools can you use to align, align, and align?

_____
_____
_____
_____
_____
_____
_____
_____
_____
_____
_____
_____

And so it is!

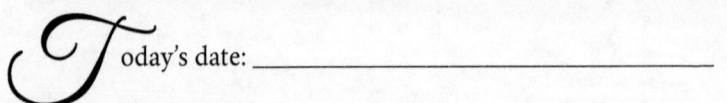oday's date: _____

Start your sentence with: "I would give anything for..." and complete it with what you want and won't be denied for today. Be clear, write with an open heart, a smile, and ecstatic excitement.

_____
_____
_____
_____
_____

Start your sentence with: "I would give anything for..." and complete it with what you want and won't be denied for your far and near future—you know, the incredible big stuff you wish for.

_____
_____
_____
_____
_____

Time for night-night gratitude! Write down what went great today by starting your sentence with: "I am grateful for..." then add the good stuff and expect a night of sweet dreams.

_____
_____
_____
_____
_____

QUOTE

Laughter heals everything! - Jacqueline Pirtle

How much do you laugh in a day, a week, or a month? What makes you laugh, and who gets you laughing? What's your opinion on laughter being able to heal—and what do you believe it can heal? What do you do to spark your own laughter? How can you laugh more often?

_____
_____
_____
_____
_____
_____
_____
_____
_____
_____
_____
_____

And so it is!

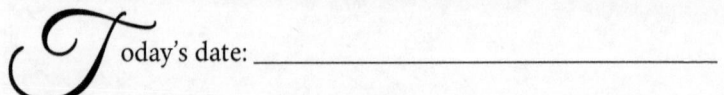oday's date: _____

Start your sentence with: "I would give anything for..." and complete it with what you want and won't be denied for today. Be clear, write with an open heart, a smile, and ecstatic excitement.

_____
_____
_____
_____
_____

Start your sentence with: "I would give anything for..." and complete it with what you want and won't be denied for your far and near future—you know, the incredible big stuff you wish for.

_____
_____
_____
_____
_____

Time for night-night gratitude! Write down what went great today by starting your sentence with: "I am grateful for..." then add the good stuff and expect a night of sweet dreams.

_____
_____
_____
_____
_____

QUOTE

Tears are like drops of gold. - Jacqueline Pirtle

Do you cry? How often and how free do you feel when you cry and after you shed your tears? What do you think about tears being drops of gold? What goodness are in tears and the act of letting them flow freely? How can you nurture your tears and celebrate them in golden ways?

_____
_____
_____
_____
_____
_____
_____
_____
_____
_____
_____
_____

And so it is!

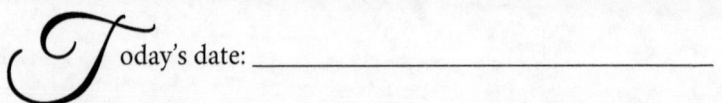oday's date: _____

Start your sentence with: "I would give anything for..." and complete it with what you want and won't be denied for today. Be clear, write with an open heart, a smile, and ecstatic excitement.

_____
_____
_____
_____
_____

Start your sentence with: "I would give anything for..." and complete it with what you want and won't be denied for your far and near future—you know, the incredible big stuff you wish for.

_____
_____
_____
_____
_____

Time for night-night gratitude! Write down what went great today by starting your sentence with: "I am grateful for..." then add the good stuff and expect a night of sweet dreams.

_____
_____
_____
_____
_____

QUOTE

Music carries you to the heavens and back. - Jacqueline Pirtle

What music do you love? How often do you listen to your favorite sounds? How do these tunes make you feel? Do you also dance when listening? How do you like your surroundings to be when you dwell in these notes—and how can you make these musical times even more special?

_____
_____
_____
_____
_____
_____
_____
_____
_____
_____
_____
_____

And so it is!

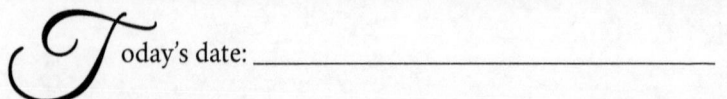oday's date: _____

Start your sentence with: "I would give anything for…" and complete it with what you want and won't be denied for today. Be clear, write with an open heart, a smile, and ecstatic excitement.

_____
_____
_____
_____
_____

Start your sentence with: "I would give anything for…" and complete it with what you want and won't be denied for your far and near future—you know, the incredible big stuff you wish for.

_____
_____
_____
_____
_____

Time for night-night gratitude! Write down what went great today by starting your sentence with: "I am grateful for…" then add the good stuff and expect a night of sweet dreams.

_____
_____
_____
_____
_____

QUOTE

Your NOW is all you got. - Jacqueline Pirtle

Do you agree? How is your NOW—okay, great, or amazing? Is it hard for you to live in the NOW? If yes, how can you make it easier? If not, how can you trigger living in the NOW even more?

_____
_____
_____
_____
_____
_____
_____
_____
_____
_____
_____
_____
_____
_____

And so it is!

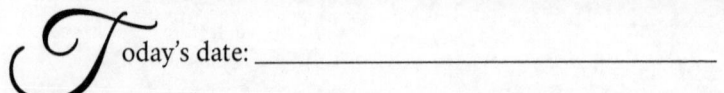oday's date: _____

START YOUR SENTENCE WITH: "I would give anything for..." and complete it with what you want and won't be denied for today. Be clear, write with an open heart, a smile, and ecstatic excitement.

_____
_____
_____
_____
_____

Start your sentence with: "I would give anything for..." and complete it with what you want and won't be denied for your far and near future—you know, the incredible big stuff you wish for.

_____
_____
_____
_____
_____

Time for night-night gratitude! Write down what went great today by starting your sentence with: "I am grateful for..." then add the good stuff and expect a night of sweet dreams.

_____
_____
_____
_____
_____

QUOTE

Rich is being and feeling abundant in every way. - Jacqueline Pirtle

How does the word "rich" make you feel? What is being rich to you—how do you look, feel, and act being rich? How can you incorporate these insights into your normal day-to-day life even if the richness of money has not shown up just yet?

_____
_____
_____
_____
_____
_____
_____
_____
_____
_____
_____
_____
_____

And so it is!

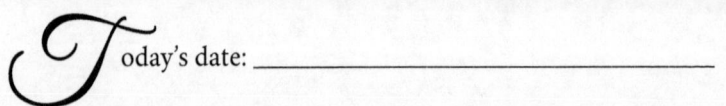oday's date: _____

Start your sentence with: "I would give anything for…" and complete it with what you want and won't be denied for today. Be clear, write with an open heart, a smile, and ecstatic excitement.

_____
_____
_____
_____
_____

Start your sentence with: "I would give anything for…" and complete it with what you want and won't be denied for your far and near future—you know, the incredible big stuff you wish for.

_____
_____
_____
_____
_____

Time for night-night gratitude! Write down what went great today by starting your sentence with: "I am grateful for…" then add the good stuff and expect a night of sweet dreams.

_____
_____
_____
_____
_____

QUOTE

Health is created in your mind. - Jacqueline Pirtle

Do you believe that? If yes, what thoughts do you have that create health or un-health for you? If not, why do you not believe it—what creates health and un-health for you? No matter your beliefs, how can you create a healthier life for yourself?

_____
_____
_____
_____
_____
_____
_____
_____
_____
_____
_____
_____
_____

And so it is!

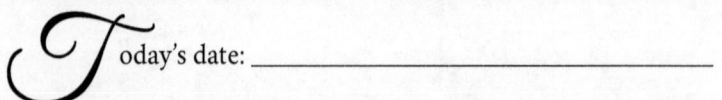oday's date: _____

START YOUR SENTENCE WITH: "I would give anything for…" and complete it with what you want and won't be denied for today. Be clear, write with an open heart, a smile, and ecstatic excitement.

_____
_____
_____
_____
_____

Start your sentence with: "I would give anything for…" and complete it with what you want and won't be denied for your far and near future—you know, the incredible big stuff you wish for.

_____
_____
_____
_____
_____

Time for night-night gratitude! Write down what went great today by starting your sentence with: "I am grateful for…" then add the good stuff and expect a night of sweet dreams.

_____
_____
_____
_____
_____

QUOTE

Feeling strong means you ARE strong. - Jacqueline Pirtle

How do you feel; strong or not? What does being strong feel like, what does it look like, and how do you act when strong? To see the contrast, how does "not strong" feel and look like? How does your "not strong" you act and show up? What tools can you apply to feel stronger every day and be the strongest you ever?

_____
_____
_____
_____
_____
_____
_____
_____
_____
_____
_____
_____

And so it is!

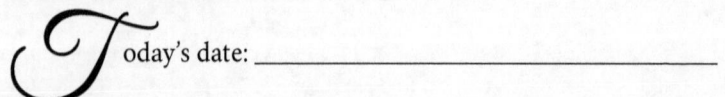
Today's date: _____

Start your sentence with: "I would give anything for…" and complete it with what you want and won't be denied for today. Be clear, write with an open heart, a smile, and ecstatic excitement.

_____
_____
_____
_____
_____

Start your sentence with: "I would give anything for…" and complete it with what you want and won't be denied for your far and near future—you know, the incredible big stuff you wish for.

_____
_____
_____
_____
_____

Time for night-night gratitude! Write down what went great today by starting your sentence with: "I am grateful for…" then add the good stuff and expect a night of sweet dreams.

_____
_____
_____
_____
_____

QUOTE

Feeling hungry is feeling alive. - Jacqueline Pirtle

When are you hungry the most? What side effects does you being hungry have—do you get angry, frustrated, sleepy, or something else? Why are you even hungry? How can you make sure to nourish yourself better and more balanced to avoid getting too hungry, but still love the feeling of hunger, while also eating the best way possible for you?

_____
_____
_____
_____
_____
_____
_____
_____
_____
_____
_____

And so it is!

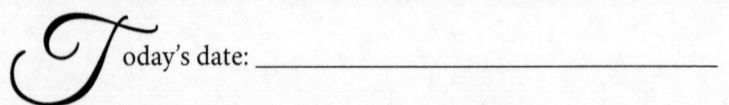 oday's date: _____

Start your sentence with: "I would give anything for…" and complete it with what you want and won't be denied for today. Be clear, write with an open heart, a smile, and ecstatic excitement.

_____
_____
_____
_____
_____

Start your sentence with: "I would give anything for…" and complete it with what you want and won't be denied for your far and near future—you know, the incredible big stuff you wish for.

_____
_____
_____
_____
_____

Time for night-night gratitude! Write down what went great today by starting your sentence with: "I am grateful for…" then add the good stuff and expect a night of sweet dreams.

_____
_____
_____
_____
_____

QUOTE

The wheels go round and round, unless you hit the brakes.
- Jacqueline Pirtle

Imagine your life as a wheel going round and round until you hit the brakes. What are your personal brakes that initiate a complete halt of living fully? Do you like your brakes that halt everything? If yes, do you still need these brakes or are they like an old safety blanket? If not, what could you do instead, to keep the flow of your life going? Also, why are you hitting those brakes; when are you using them; and how does it feel when it all stops?

_____
_____
_____
_____
_____
_____
_____

And so it is!

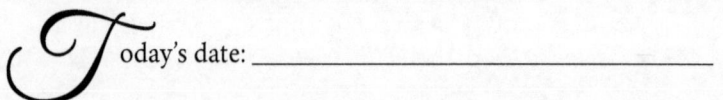oday's date: _____

Start your sentence with: "I would give anything for…" and complete it with what you want and won't be denied for today. Be clear, write with an open heart, a smile, and ecstatic excitement.

_____
_____
_____
_____
_____

Start your sentence with: "I would give anything for…" and complete it with what you want and won't be denied for your far and near future—you know, the incredible big stuff you wish for.

_____
_____
_____
_____
_____

Time for night-night gratitude! Write down what went great today by starting your sentence with: "I am grateful for…" then add the good stuff and expect a night of sweet dreams.

_____
_____
_____
_____
_____

QUOTE

Parachutes are lifesavers! - Jacqueline Pirtle

What or who is your parachute in life, gathering you before it's too late? What could you do to not need a parachute in certain situations, or less at times? Helping others in need, being their parachute, is a potent energy—how can you support others more often?

_____
_____
_____
_____
_____
_____
_____
_____
_____
_____
_____
_____

And so it is!

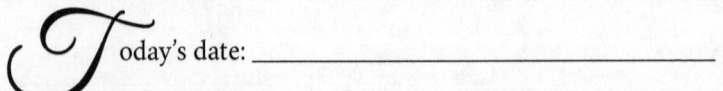 Today's date: _____

Start your sentence with: "I would give anything for..." and complete it with what you want and won't be denied for today. Be clear, write with an open heart, a smile, and ecstatic excitement.

_____
_____
_____
_____
_____

Start your sentence with: "I would give anything for..." and complete it with what you want and won't be denied for your far and near future—you know, the incredible big stuff you wish for.

_____
_____
_____
_____
_____

Time for night-night gratitude! Write down what went great today by starting your sentence with: "I am grateful for..." then add the good stuff and expect a night of sweet dreams.

_____
_____
_____
_____
_____

QUOTE

"Nothing (ever) works." Is that true or are we humans misunderstanding how life works? - Jacqueline Pirtle

What is not working for you? Why are things not going your way? Is it because you don't believe that it could work, or that it's not the right thing for you and so it won't work? Are you not giving enough of an energetic push to make clear that you want it? Dig deep here, find the cause of what is not working and why —not by blaming others or life itself, but by taking responsibility for what you are doing, feeling, or saying for it not to work.

_____
_____
_____
_____
_____
_____
_____
_____
_____

And so it is!

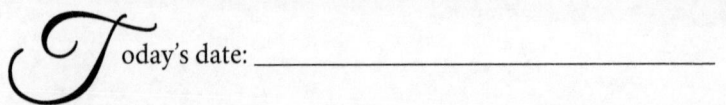 oday's date: _____

START YOUR SENTENCE WITH: "I would give anything for…" and complete it with what you want and won't be denied for today. Be clear, write with an open heart, a smile, and ecstatic excitement.

_____
_____
_____
_____
_____

Start your sentence with: "I would give anything for…" and complete it with what you want and won't be denied for your far and near future—you know, the incredible big stuff you wish for.

_____
_____
_____
_____
_____

Time for night-night gratitude! Write down what went great today by starting your sentence with: "I am grateful for…" then add the good stuff and expect a night of sweet dreams.

_____
_____
_____
_____
_____

QUOTE

Everything happens for you, never to you. - Jacqueline Pirtle

What in your life do you feel is happening *to* you? Make your list, then go through it one by one, changing your attitude to: "This is happening for me, so what does this mean for me; what lesson is there for me, and what gold can I take away from this?"

_____
_____
_____
_____
_____
_____
_____
_____
_____
_____
_____
_____
_____

And so it is!

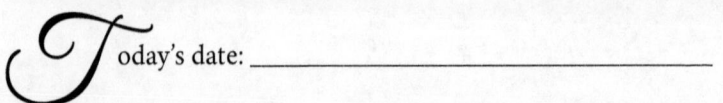Today's date: _____

START YOUR SENTENCE WITH: "I would give anything for…" and complete it with what you want and won't be denied for today. Be clear, write with an open heart, a smile, and ecstatic excitement.

_____
_____
_____
_____
_____

Start your sentence with: "I would give anything for…" and complete it with what you want and won't be denied for your far and near future—you know, the incredible big stuff you wish for.

_____
_____
_____
_____
_____

Time for night-night gratitude! Write down what went great today by starting your sentence with: "I am grateful for…" then add the good stuff and expect a night of sweet dreams.

_____
_____
_____
_____
_____

QUOTE

The sun! She rises every day no matter what. - Jacqueline Pirtle

How can you rise like the sun, every day, no matter what? What's the outcome when you base how you show up on what you want in life—versus focusing on what you don't want or feeling down about life? Most importantly, what's your strategy to commit to being you—every single new day?

_____
_____
_____
_____
_____
_____
_____
_____
_____
_____
_____
_____

And so it is!

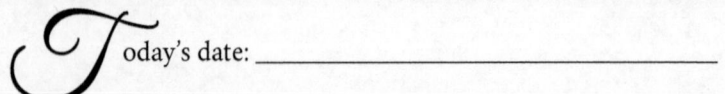

Today's date: _____

Start your sentence with: "I would give anything for…" and complete it with what you want and won't be denied for today. Be clear, write with an open heart, a smile, and ecstatic excitement.

_____
_____
_____
_____
_____

Start your sentence with: "I would give anything for…" and complete it with what you want and won't be denied for your far and near future—you know, the incredible big stuff you wish for.

_____
_____
_____
_____
_____

Time for night-night gratitude! Write down what went great today by starting your sentence with: "I am grateful for…" then add the good stuff and expect a night of sweet dreams.

_____
_____
_____
_____
_____

QUOTE

When in Rome...

Finish the sentence with glorious perspectives of living "la dolce vita." Now implement THAT into your new day, enjoying a fabulous you in Rome. What is that lifestyle of yours going to look like? What are you wearing, how are you smiling, moving, and living? Go on, be the excitement today!

_____
_____
_____
_____
_____
_____
_____
_____
_____
_____
_____
_____

And so it is!

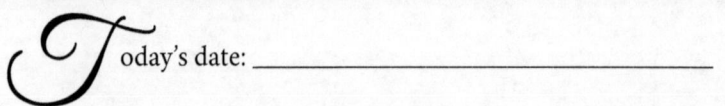oday's date: _____

Start your sentence with: "I would give anything for..." and complete it with what you want and won't be denied for today. Be clear, write with an open heart, a smile, and ecstatic excitement.

_____
_____
_____
_____
_____

Start your sentence with: "I would give anything for..." and complete it with what you want and won't be denied for your far and near future—you know, the incredible big stuff you wish for.

_____
_____
_____
_____
_____

Time for night-night gratitude! Write down what went great today by starting your sentence with: "I am grateful for..." then add the good stuff and expect a night of sweet dreams.

_____
_____
_____
_____
_____

QUOTE

Kindness never fails. - Jacqueline Pirtle

What is kindness to you? How does it feel—what impact does being kind have? How can you be kinder to yourself and others? Make your kind plan.

_____
_____
_____
_____
_____
_____
_____
_____
_____
_____
_____
_____
_____

And so it is!

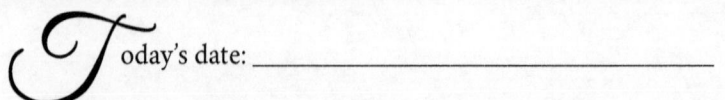oday's date: _____

Start your sentence with: "I would give anything for…" and complete it with what you want and won't be denied for today. Be clear, write with an open heart, a smile, and ecstatic excitement.

_____
_____
_____
_____
_____

Start your sentence with: "I would give anything for…" and complete it with what you want and won't be denied for your far and near future—you know, the incredible big stuff you wish for.

_____
_____
_____
_____
_____

Time for night-night gratitude! Write down what went great today by starting your sentence with: "I am grateful for…" then add the good stuff and expect a night of sweet dreams.

_____
_____
_____
_____
_____

QUOTE

Dreams are only dreams until you decide that they are your reality.
- Jacqueline Pirtle

What are your dreams? Why are they just dreams, and what is keeping them from being real? How can you make your deepest desires your reality?

_____
_____
_____
_____
_____
_____
_____
_____
_____
_____
_____
_____
_____

And so it is!

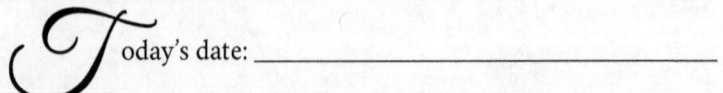Today's date: _____

START YOUR SENTENCE WITH: "I would give anything for..." and complete it with what you want and won't be denied for today. Be clear, write with an open heart, a smile, and ecstatic excitement.

_____
_____
_____
_____
_____

Start your sentence with: "I would give anything for..." and complete it with what you want and won't be denied for your far and near future—you know, the incredible big stuff you wish for.

_____
_____
_____
_____
_____

Time for night-night gratitude! Write down what went great today by starting your sentence with: "I am grateful for..." then add the good stuff and expect a night of sweet dreams.

_____
_____
_____
_____
_____

QUOTE

Worries have never solved anything; let alone helped anyone.
- Jacqueline Pirtle

Do you worry? How much and how often do you worry? Are you aware of when you worry, or realize only later when the stress about your worries has already kicked in? How can you worry less, since worries are never helpful, healthy, or real?

_____
_____
_____
_____
_____
_____
_____
_____
_____
_____
_____
_____

And so it is!

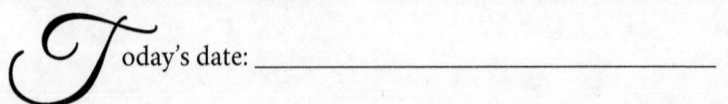

Today's date: _____

Start your sentence with: "I would give anything for…" and complete it with what you want and won't be denied for today. Be clear, write with an open heart, a smile, and ecstatic excitement.

_____
_____
_____
_____
_____

Start your sentence with: "I would give anything for…" and complete it with what you want and won't be denied for your far and near future—you know, the incredible big stuff you wish for.

_____
_____
_____
_____
_____

Time for night-night gratitude! Write down what went great today by starting your sentence with: "I am grateful for…" then add the good stuff and expect a night of sweet dreams.

_____
_____
_____
_____
_____

QUOTE

Rest assured, you will be fine. - Jacqueline Pirtle

Do you believe that you are fine—or will be fine? If yes, how can you strengthen this wonderful and lightening belief? If not, why don't you trust those words? How can you shift from not okay to knowing that you are okay, or will be okay, no matter what?

_____
_____
_____
_____
_____
_____
_____
_____
_____
_____
_____
_____

And so it is!

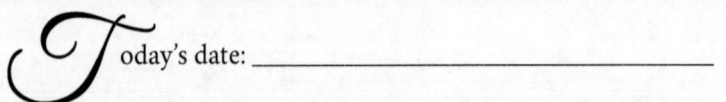oday's date: _____

Start your sentence with: "I would give anything for..." and complete it with what you want and won't be denied for today. Be clear, write with an open heart, a smile, and ecstatic excitement.

_____
_____
_____
_____
_____

Start your sentence with: "I would give anything for..." and complete it with what you want and won't be denied for your far and near future—you know, the incredible big stuff you wish for.

_____
_____
_____
_____
_____

Time for night-night gratitude! Write down what went great today by starting your sentence with: "I am grateful for..." then add the good stuff and expect a night of sweet dreams.

_____
_____
_____
_____
_____

QUOTE

Nothing ever stays the same, everything is always changing and new—so why not wait things out? - Jacqueline Pirtle

How can you pause your brain a bit more to let life change things for you—instead of changing everything by yourself and crumbling under the exhaustion of solving things alone, creating the feeling that you are lost?

_____
_____
_____
_____
_____
_____
_____
_____
_____
_____
_____
_____

And so it is!

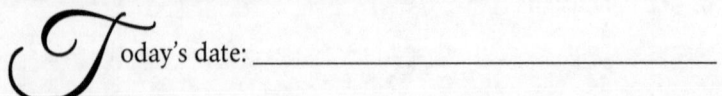Today's date: _____

Start your sentence with: "I would give anything for..." and complete it with what you want and won't be denied for today. Be clear, write with an open heart, a smile, and ecstatic excitement.

_____
_____
_____
_____
_____

Start your sentence with: "I would give anything for..." and complete it with what you want and won't be denied for your far and near future—you know, the incredible big stuff you wish for.

_____
_____
_____
_____
_____

Time for night-night gratitude! Write down what went great today by starting your sentence with: "I am grateful for..." then add the good stuff and expect a night of sweet dreams.

_____
_____
_____
_____
_____

QUOTE

What's this gotta do with you? A lot! - Jacqueline Pirtle

Everything that's in your awareness has to do with you—always! Asking yourself "what does this have to do with me?" opens a treasure chest of wisdom, which you can take to heart and act on. What are some tough situations in your life right now that you need to understand?

_____
_____
_____
_____
_____
_____
_____
_____
_____
_____
_____
_____

And so it is!

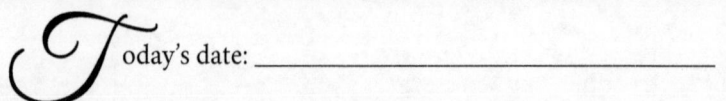 oday's date: _____

START YOUR SENTENCE WITH: "I would give anything for…" and complete it with what you want and won't be denied for today. Be clear, write with an open heart, a smile, and ecstatic excitement.

_____
_____
_____
_____
_____

Start your sentence with: "I would give anything for…" and complete it with what you want and won't be denied for your far and near future—you know, the incredible big stuff you wish for.

_____
_____
_____
_____
_____

Time for night-night gratitude! Write down what went great today by starting your sentence with: "I am grateful for…" then add the good stuff and expect a night of sweet dreams.

_____
_____
_____
_____
_____

QUOTE

If you think you can't, then you can't. - Jacqueline Pirtle

How can you think "I can" more often, so that you actually and truly can? What plan can you come up with to become an I-can believer?

_____
_____
_____
_____
_____
_____
_____
_____
_____
_____
_____
_____
_____

And so it is!

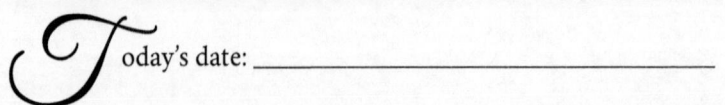oday's date: _____

Start your sentence with: "I would give anything for..." and complete it with what you want and won't be denied for today. Be clear, write with an open heart, a smile, and ecstatic excitement.

_____
_____
_____
_____
_____

Start your sentence with: "I would give anything for..." and complete it with what you want and won't be denied for your far and near future—you know, the incredible big stuff you wish for.

_____
_____
_____
_____
_____

Time for night-night gratitude! Write down what went great today by starting your sentence with: "I am grateful for..." then add the good stuff and expect a night of sweet dreams.

_____
_____
_____
_____
_____

QUOTE

Any lie can be turned into a truth. - Jacqueline Pirtle

How many times have you done something regardless of if you wanted to do it? How often have you made up reasons to not participate or go out? How normal is it for you to think one thing but do, say, or feel something else? Really become aware of how unaligned you are in these moments and turn these little - or sometimes big - lies into your truth, creating an aligned state in which you can boldly speak up.

_____
_____
_____
_____
_____
_____
_____
_____
_____
_____

And so it is!

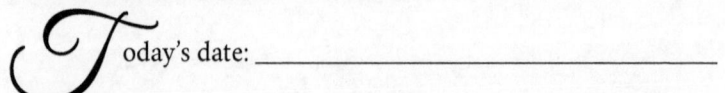

Today's date: _____

Start your sentence with: "I would give anything for..." and complete it with what you want and won't be denied for today. Be clear, write with an open heart, a smile, and ecstatic excitement.

_____
_____
_____
_____
_____

Start your sentence with: "I would give anything for..." and complete it with what you want and won't be denied for your far and near future—you know, the incredible big stuff you wish for.

_____
_____
_____
_____
_____

Time for night-night gratitude! Write down what went great today by starting your sentence with: "I am grateful for..." then add the good stuff and expect a night of sweet dreams.

_____
_____
_____
_____
_____

QUOTE

Not all spaghetti are alike! - Jacqueline Pirtle

You are unique, even though you are a person just like everyone else. What makes you unique, what is your own style of spaghetti?

_____
_____
_____
_____
_____
_____
_____
_____
_____
_____
_____
_____
_____
_____

And so it is!

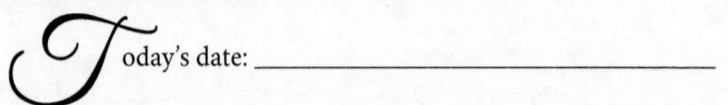Today's date: _____

Start your sentence with: "I would give anything for..." and complete it with what you want and won't be denied for today. Be clear, write with an open heart, a smile, and ecstatic excitement.

_____
_____
_____
_____
_____

Start your sentence with: "I would give anything for..." and complete it with what you want and won't be denied for your far and near future—you know, the incredible big stuff you wish for.

_____
_____
_____
_____
_____

Time for night-night gratitude! Write down what went great today by starting your sentence with: "I am grateful for..." then add the good stuff and expect a night of sweet dreams.

_____
_____
_____
_____
_____

QUOTE

Your outer-life mirrors you your inner-life. - Jacqueline Pirtle

What does your life look like—what is working, and what is not? Look around, take inventory, and make your outer-life list. Then take what is not working and realize it as your mirror—showing you what is upside-down inside of you. How can you make it upside-right inside of you?

_____
_____
_____
_____
_____
_____
_____
_____
_____
_____
_____

And so it is!

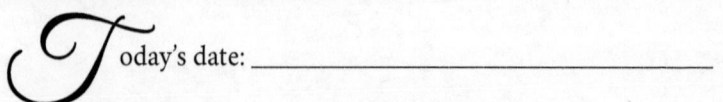oday's date: _____

Start your sentence with: "I would give anything for…" and complete it with what you want and won't be denied for today. Be clear, write with an open heart, a smile, and ecstatic excitement.

_____
_____
_____
_____
_____

Start your sentence with: "I would give anything for…" and complete it with what you want and won't be denied for your far and near future—you know, the incredible big stuff you wish for.

_____
_____
_____
_____
_____

Time for night-night gratitude! Write down what went great today by starting your sentence with: "I am grateful for…" then add the good stuff and expect a night of sweet dreams.

_____
_____
_____
_____
_____

QUOTE

Prioritizing feeling well is a straight line to happiness.
- Jacqueline Pirtle

What is your priority: To get stuff done, help everyone else, be a good person, or to feel well, be healthy, successful, abundant? Do you struggle with feeling good at times while focusing on any of these priorities? If yes, why is that so—and how can you prioritize feeling well more often? If not, how good do you actually feel—and could you feel even better?

_____
_____
_____
_____
_____
_____
_____
_____
_____
_____

And so it is!

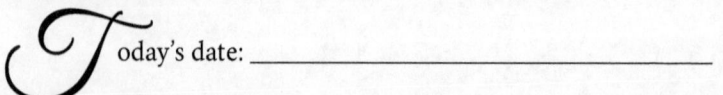oday's date: _____

START YOUR SENTENCE WITH: "I would give anything for..." and complete it with what you want and won't be denied for today. Be clear, write with an open heart, a smile, and ecstatic excitement.

_____
_____
_____
_____
_____

Start your sentence with: "I would give anything for..." and complete it with what you want and won't be denied for your far and near future—you know, the incredible big stuff you wish for.

_____
_____
_____
_____
_____

Time for night-night gratitude! Write down what went great today by starting your sentence with: "I am grateful for..." then add the good stuff and expect a night of sweet dreams.

_____
_____
_____
_____
_____

QUOTE

Rebelling means one does not want it because one does not align with it.
- Jacqueline Pirtle

When do you rebel and what are you rebelling against? Since rebelling is a barometer of alignment - showing you wether you are in your true alignment or not - how can you embrace your rebellions and those of others fully and completely?

_____
_____
_____
_____
_____
_____
_____
_____
_____
_____
_____

And so it is!

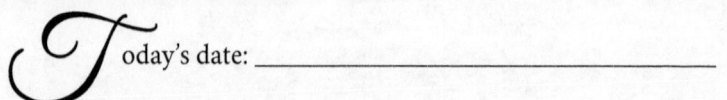Today's date: _____

Start your sentence with: "I would give anything for…" and complete it with what you want and won't be denied for today. Be clear, write with an open heart, a smile, and ecstatic excitement.

_____
_____
_____
_____
_____

Start your sentence with: "I would give anything for…" and complete it with what you want and won't be denied for your far and near future—you know, the incredible big stuff you wish for.

_____
_____
_____
_____
_____

Time for night-night gratitude! Write down what went great today by starting your sentence with: "I am grateful for…" then add the good stuff and expect a night of sweet dreams.

_____
_____
_____
_____
_____

QUOTE

Relationships are playgrounds in disguise. - Jacqueline Pirtle

Where is your truth in these words, and do you think playing can change the world by creating more harmony? Are you playing in your relationships—which ones are a yes, and which are the no's? How can you play more often in your relationship with yourself and others?

_____
_____
_____
_____
_____
_____
_____
_____
_____
_____
_____

And so it is!

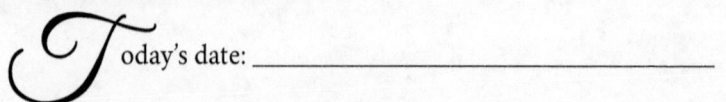Today's date: _____

Start your sentence with: "I would give anything for…" and complete it with what you want and won't be denied for today. Be clear, write with an open heart, a smile, and ecstatic excitement.

_____
_____
_____
_____
_____

Start your sentence with: "I would give anything for…" and complete it with what you want and won't be denied for your far and near future—you know, the incredible big stuff you wish for.

_____
_____
_____
_____
_____

Time for night-night gratitude! Write down what went great today by starting your sentence with: "I am grateful for…" then add the good stuff and expect a night of sweet dreams.

_____
_____
_____
_____
_____

QUOTE

Say, think, hear, see, feel, smell, taste, do... Let's go! - Jacqueline Pirtle

Reading these words initiate a feeling, but maybe also a vision. So, what's on your mind, and go where? What's holding you back from speeding towards what you feel pulled to—is there anything holding you back saying "stop"? How will your day change by using "Let's go!" as your mantra? How can you apply the energy behind this short but potent phrase as your fuel for the best day ever?

_____
_____
_____
_____
_____
_____
_____
_____
_____
_____

And so it is!

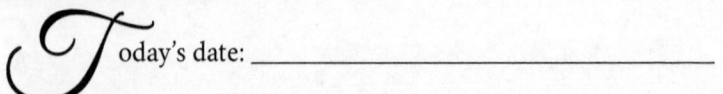

Today's date: _____

Start your sentence with: "I would give anything for…" and complete it with what you want and won't be denied for today. Be clear, write with an open heart, a smile, and ecstatic excitement.

_____
_____
_____
_____
_____

Start your sentence with: "I would give anything for…" and complete it with what you want and won't be denied for your far and near future—you know, the incredible big stuff you wish for.

_____
_____
_____
_____
_____

Time for night-night gratitude! Write down what went great today by starting your sentence with: "I am grateful for…" then add the good stuff and expect a night of sweet dreams.

_____
_____
_____
_____
_____

QUOTE

Happiness is being YOU! - Jacqueline Pirtle

How happy are you? When are you happiest—or unhappiest? When being YOU, are you happy? If yes, how does being you look like—how do you do YOU? If not, what is the unhappy about and how could you truly be you, so you can be a happy you?

_____
_____
_____
_____
_____
_____
_____
_____
_____
_____
_____
_____
_____

And so it is!

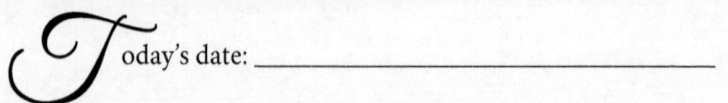oday's date: _____

Start your sentence with: "I would give anything for..." and complete it with what you want and won't be denied for today. Be clear, write with an open heart, a smile, and ecstatic excitement.

_____
_____
_____
_____
_____

Start your sentence with: "I would give anything for..." and complete it with what you want and won't be denied for your far and near future—you know, the incredible big stuff you wish for.

_____
_____
_____
_____
_____

Time for night-night gratitude! Write down what went great today by starting your sentence with: "I am grateful for..." then add the good stuff and expect a night of sweet dreams.

_____
_____
_____
_____
_____

QUOTE

Home is where your heart is. - Jacqueline Pirtle

Where is your heart and what stole your heart—place and time wise? Describe how you feel with your heart being there.

Now touch your heart, close your eyes, and breathe—realize that even though you said your heart is somewhere, it actually is inside of you, meaning that you are always home as long as you feel your heart right there with you. Any thoughts on that?

_____
_____
_____
_____
_____
_____
_____
_____
_____
_____
_____

And so it is!

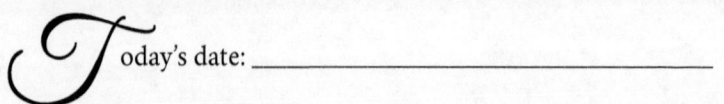Today's date: _____

Start your sentence with: "I would give anything for…" and complete it with what you want and won't be denied for today. Be clear, write with an open heart, a smile, and ecstatic excitement.

_____
_____
_____
_____
_____

Start your sentence with: "I would give anything for…" and complete it with what you want and won't be denied for your far and near future—you know, the incredible big stuff you wish for.

_____
_____
_____
_____
_____

Time for night-night gratitude! Write down what went great today by starting your sentence with: "I am grateful for…" then add the good stuff and expect a night of sweet dreams.

_____
_____
_____
_____
_____

QUOTE

Flower blooms are like feeling detonators, keeping you awake and entertained through your senses. - Jacqueline Pirtle

What are your favorite flower blooms? What colors are they, how do they smell, and what emotions do they grant you? How could you integrate blooms and the presence they are into your brilliant new day ahead?

_____
_____
_____
_____
_____
_____
_____
_____
_____
_____
_____
_____

And so it is!

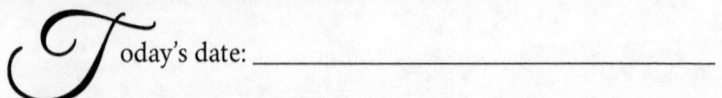Today's date: _____

Start your sentence with: "I would give anything for..." and complete it with what you want and won't be denied for today. Be clear, write with an open heart, a smile, and ecstatic excitement.

_____
_____
_____
_____
_____

Start your sentence with: "I would give anything for..." and complete it with what you want and won't be denied for your far and near future—you know, the incredible big stuff you wish for.

_____
_____
_____
_____
_____

Time for night-night gratitude! Write down what went great today by starting your sentence with: "I am grateful for..." then add the good stuff and expect a night of sweet dreams.

_____
_____
_____
_____
_____

QUOTE

Your senses are deliberately trying to get you to experience beauty.
- Jacqueline Pirtle

What is beauty to you—and how important is beauty to you? How does prettiness make you feel? Look around you, smell all there is, hear what's going on, taste the world, and touch whatever you can—how much beauty can you find? How do you feel being aware of so much loveliness? Could you create more gorgeousness for yourself?

_____
_____
_____
_____
_____
_____
_____
_____
_____
_____

And so it is!

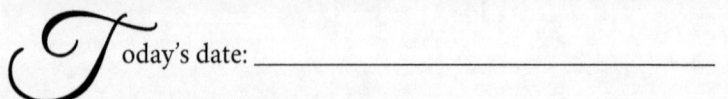 Today's date: _____

Start your sentence with: "I would give anything for…" and complete it with what you want and won't be denied for today. Be clear, write with an open heart, a smile, and ecstatic excitement.

_____
_____
_____
_____
_____

Start your sentence with: "I would give anything for…" and complete it with what you want and won't be denied for your far and near future—you know, the incredible big stuff you wish for.

_____
_____
_____
_____
_____

Time for night-night gratitude! Write down what went great today by starting your sentence with: "I am grateful for…" then add the good stuff and expect a night of sweet dreams.

_____
_____
_____
_____
_____

QUOTE

Asking questions initiates answers and those answers are the antidotes to all worries—besides you not walking the earth clueless and uninformed. - Jacqueline Pirtle

Do you like asking questions? What are your favorite questions to ask? Who do you like asking a lot? How do you feel asking so many questions—could you ask even more, to enjoy even more clarity? How can you feel freer to ask, ask, and ask even more?

_____
_____
_____
_____
_____
_____
_____
_____
_____
_____

And so it is!

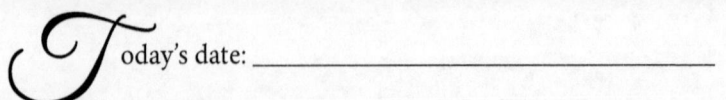 oday's date: _____

START YOUR SENTENCE WITH: "I would give anything for…" and complete it with what you want and won't be denied for today. Be clear, write with an open heart, a smile, and ecstatic excitement.

_____
_____
_____
_____
_____

Start your sentence with: "I would give anything for…" and complete it with what you want and won't be denied for your far and near future—you know, the incredible big stuff you wish for.

_____
_____
_____
_____
_____

Time for night-night gratitude! Write down what went great today by starting your sentence with: "I am grateful for…" then add the good stuff and expect a night of sweet dreams.

_____
_____
_____
_____
_____

QUOTE

Breathing is life. - Jacqueline Pirtle

Every breath in means you fill yourself with oxygen and every breath out cleanses your gunk out—energetically, mentally, emotionally, and physically.

How deep do you normally breathe? Be honest here.

Now take the deepest breath ever—how does it feel to stretch your lungs in such grand ways?

Next, come up with ways to remind yourself in your busy days to fill those lungs of yours to feel alive and full of energy.

_____
_____
_____
_____
_____
_____
_____
_____

And so it is!

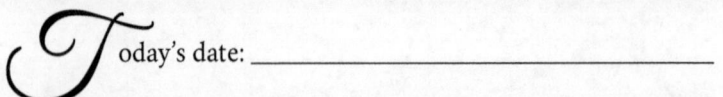 oday's date: _____

START YOUR SENTENCE WITH: "I would give anything for…" and complete it with what you want and won't be denied for today. Be clear, write with an open heart, a smile, and ecstatic excitement.

_____
_____
_____
_____
_____

Start your sentence with: "I would give anything for…" and complete it with what you want and won't be denied for your far and near future—you know, the incredible big stuff you wish for.

_____
_____
_____
_____
_____

Time for night-night gratitude! Write down what went great today by starting your sentence with: "I am grateful for…" then add the good stuff and expect a night of sweet dreams.

_____
_____
_____
_____
_____

QUOTE

Smiling changes everything; your energy, your physics, thoughts, feelings, health, happiness, and success. Literally the whole of you gets changed. - Jacqueline Pirtle

Lift your lips into a grin. How changed do you feel? Now make a grunting face, lips down—how do you feel? Then make a straight line with your beautiful lips, what emotions does this straightness fill you with? How can you be more aware of the power of your lips and what keeps them upturned more often?

_____
_____
_____
_____
_____
_____
_____
_____
_____
_____

And so it is!

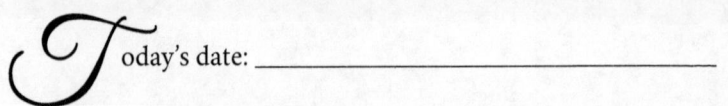oday's date: _____

START YOUR SENTENCE WITH: "I would give anything for..." and complete it with what you want and won't be denied for today. Be clear, write with an open heart, a smile, and ecstatic excitement.

_____
_____
_____
_____
_____

Start your sentence with: "I would give anything for..." and complete it with what you want and won't be denied for your far and near future—you know, the incredible big stuff you wish for.

_____
_____
_____
_____
_____

Time for night-night gratitude! Write down what went great today by starting your sentence with: "I am grateful for..." then add the good stuff and expect a night of sweet dreams.

_____
_____
_____
_____
_____

QUOTE

The cherry on top matters! - Jacqueline Pirtle

What does the cherry on top make you feel? What represents the cherry on top for you in everything; life, food, emotions, thoughts, adventures, and experiences? How can you create more cherries to top your world in every split second?

_____
_____
_____
_____
_____
_____
_____
_____
_____
_____
_____
_____
_____

And so it is!

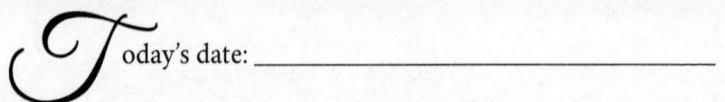oday's date: _____

Start your sentence with: "I would give anything for…" and complete it with what you want and won't be denied for today. Be clear, write with an open heart, a smile, and ecstatic excitement.

_____
_____
_____
_____
_____

Start your sentence with: "I would give anything for…" and complete it with what you want and won't be denied for your far and near future—you know, the incredible big stuff you wish for.

_____
_____
_____
_____
_____

Time for night-night gratitude! Write down what went great today by starting your sentence with: "I am grateful for…" then add the good stuff and expect a night of sweet dreams.

_____
_____
_____
_____
_____

QUOTE

Wondering is like a stairway, getting you to what is possible.
- Jacqueline Pirtle

Do you wonder like a child wonders; do you feel the moment when wondering creates magick and hope? If yes, how do you feel wondering away, and how could you wonder even bigger and more often? If not, can you watch a child—or even better, learn from a child?

_____
_____
_____
_____
_____
_____
_____
_____
_____
_____

And so it is!

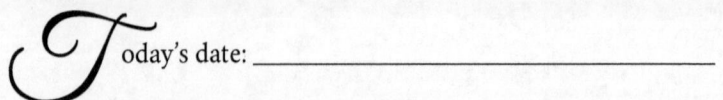

Today's date: _____

Start your sentence with: "I would give anything for..." and complete it with what you want and won't be denied for today. Be clear, write with an open heart, a smile, and ecstatic excitement.

_____
_____
_____
_____
_____

Start your sentence with: "I would give anything for..." and complete it with what you want and won't be denied for your far and near future—you know, the incredible big stuff you wish for.

_____
_____
_____
_____
_____

Time for night-night gratitude! Write down what went great today by starting your sentence with: "I am grateful for..." then add the good stuff and expect a night of sweet dreams.

_____
_____
_____
_____
_____

QUOTE

Rain puddles invite dance and play. - Jacqueline Pirtle

What is your first reaction when it rains, when the puddles are just starting to form? Do you get the nudge to go out and jump, dance, and play in them—co-creating a field of creativity and laughter with this wet mess? If yes, how can you be more aware of that uplift happening next time it rains? If not, when are you going to buy yourself some rain boots to at least try?

_____
_____
_____
_____
_____
_____
_____
_____
_____
_____

And so it is!

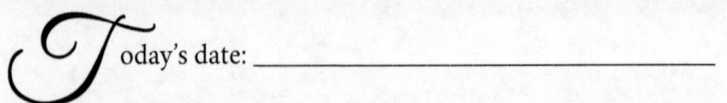oday's date: _____

Start your sentence with: "I would give anything for..." and complete it with what you want and won't be denied for today. Be clear, write with an open heart, a smile, and ecstatic excitement.

_____
_____
_____
_____
_____

Start your sentence with: "I would give anything for..." and complete it with what you want and won't be denied for your far and near future—you know, the incredible big stuff you wish for.

_____
_____
_____
_____
_____

Time for night-night gratitude! Write down what went great today by starting your sentence with: "I am grateful for..." then add the good stuff and expect a night of sweet dreams.

_____
_____
_____
_____
_____

QUOTE

Shoes are strong and powerful; they carry you through your day.
- Jacqueline Pirtle

What energy do your shoes carry—sport shoes are sporty, fast, and light; high heels are elegant, highly, and queen like; flats are playful, light, and summery; hiking boots are powerful, strong, and capable; sandals are free, airy, and fun... Get to the bottom of the shoes you own!

How do you choose your shoes for your day, or the moment —in the flash, quickly, or with the awareness of how you feel in certain shoes? Can you take some time to connect with your shoes before you put them on, to make sure you're aligned with the energy carrying you through your day?

_____
_____
_____
_____
_____

And so it is!

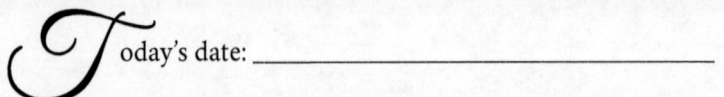 oday's date: _____

Start your sentence with: "I would give anything for..." and complete it with what you want and won't be denied for today. Be clear, write with an open heart, a smile, and ecstatic excitement.

_____
_____
_____
_____
_____

Start your sentence with: "I would give anything for..." and complete it with what you want and won't be denied for your far and near future—you know, the incredible big stuff you wish for.

_____
_____
_____
_____
_____

Time for night-night gratitude! Write down what went great today by starting your sentence with: "I am grateful for..." then add the good stuff and expect a night of sweet dreams.

_____
_____
_____
_____
_____

QUOTE

Water is not only hydration, it holds information and makes up a main part of you physically—oh, and it's also a pro at being in the flow.
- Jacqueline Pirtle

How hydrated are you; do you feel moisturized, and are you drinking enough? What attention do you give water - before you drink it, when it comes out the faucet, or when it's in front of you - do you mindlessly drink it, let it go down the drain just like that, or are you mindfully feeling its flow? Do you bless it with gratitude and happiness before it enters your body—filling it with the highest and most beautiful energy to get the best of what water has to offer you?

_____
_____
_____
_____
_____
_____

And so it is!

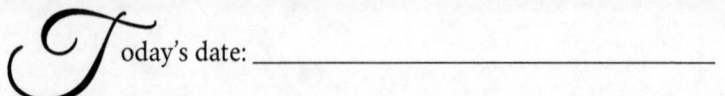

Today's date: _____

START YOUR SENTENCE WITH: "I would give anything for..." and complete it with what you want and won't be denied for today. Be clear, write with an open heart, a smile, and ecstatic excitement.

_____
_____
_____
_____
_____

Start your sentence with: "I would give anything for..." and complete it with what you want and won't be denied for your far and near future—you know, the incredible big stuff you wish for.

_____
_____
_____
_____
_____

Time for night-night gratitude! Write down what went great today by starting your sentence with: "I am grateful for..." then add the good stuff and expect a night of sweet dreams.

_____
_____
_____
_____
_____

QUOTE

Rainbows are for dreamers. - Jacqueline Pirtle

Do you like rainbows? If yes, you are a natural dreamer—question is what do you like about them, how do they make you feel, and what is the inspiration behind them? If not, what's not to like about them and how could you start liking them, and take the nudge to be a professional dreamer?

_____
_____
_____
_____
_____
_____
_____
_____
_____
_____
_____

And so it is!

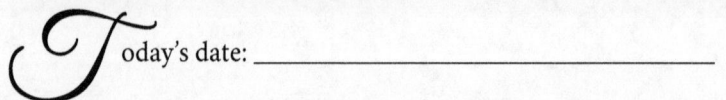oday's date: _____

Start your sentence with: "I would give anything for..." and complete it with what you want and won't be denied for today. Be clear, write with an open heart, a smile, and ecstatic excitement.

_____
_____
_____
_____
_____

Start your sentence with: "I would give anything for..." and complete it with what you want and won't be denied for your far and near future—you know, the incredible big stuff you wish for.

_____
_____
_____
_____
_____

Time for night-night gratitude! Write down what went great today by starting your sentence with: "I am grateful for..." then add the good stuff and expect a night of sweet dreams.

_____
_____
_____
_____
_____

QUOTE

Sweet is what touches and moves your heart. - Jacqueline Pirtle

How's your heart doing—how is it feeling? Could it use more touching and moving? What touches and moves your love machine in huge ways, and how can you create self-love-waves in your heart?

_____
_____
_____
_____
_____
_____
_____
_____
_____
_____
_____
_____

And so it is!

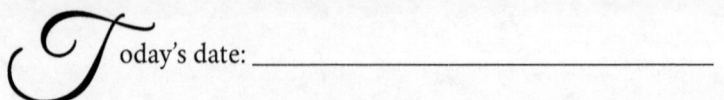Today's date: _____

Start your sentence with: "I would give anything for..." and complete it with what you want and won't be denied for today. Be clear, write with an open heart, a smile, and ecstatic excitement.

_____
_____
_____
_____
_____

Start your sentence with: "I would give anything for..." and complete it with what you want and won't be denied for your far and near future—you know, the incredible big stuff you wish for.

_____
_____
_____
_____
_____

Time for night night-gratitude! Write down what went great today by starting your sentence with: "I am grateful for..." then add the good stuff and expect a night of sweet dreams.

_____
_____
_____
_____
_____

QUOTE

There is adventure in every single weather situation, and that should get your excitement and creativity sparking. - Jacqueline Pirtle

What is your favorite weather—and why? What do you wear in your preferred weather situation—how does it make you feel? Now on to the not-so-loved weather conditions: why are you not a fan, how could you see the adventure in them anyways?

_____
_____
_____
_____
_____
_____
_____
_____
_____
_____
_____
_____

And so it is!

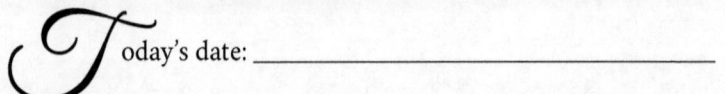Today's date: _____

Start your sentence with: "I would give anything for…" and complete it with what you want and won't be denied for today. Be clear, write with an open heart, a smile, and ecstatic excitement.

_____
_____
_____
_____
_____

Start your sentence with: "I would give anything for…" and complete it with what you want and won't be denied for your far and near future—you know, the incredible big stuff you wish for.

_____
_____
_____
_____
_____

Time for night-night gratitude! Write down what went great today by starting your sentence with: "I am grateful for…" then add the good stuff and expect a night of sweet dreams.

_____
_____
_____
_____
_____

QUOTE

Sitting in misery is a way of giving up. - Jacqueline Pirtle

Feeling miserable is okay and normal. The question is, what are you doing when all things horrible hit the fan? Are you cluelessly giving in, not knowing what to do? Or are you embracing this human moment, to right after shift your direction towards feeling better? How can you claim power over your moods—which in reality are only old habits, here to be overridden?

_____
_____
_____
_____
_____
_____
_____
_____
_____
_____

And so it is!

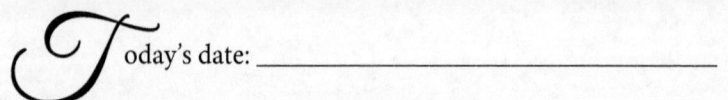oday's date: _____

Start your sentence with: "I would give anything for..." and complete it with what you want and won't be denied for today. Be clear, write with an open heart, a smile, and ecstatic excitement.

_____
_____
_____
_____
_____

Start your sentence with: "I would give anything for..." and complete it with what you want and won't be denied for your far and near future—you know, the incredible big stuff you wish for.

_____
_____
_____
_____
_____

Time for night-night gratitude! Write down what went great today by starting your sentence with: "I am grateful for..." then add the good stuff and expect a night of sweet dreams.

_____
_____
_____
_____
_____

QUOTE

"The End" has a meaning of "that's it, finish, nothing else can be done." But that's not true nor valid since everything is energy, and energy doesn't have a beginning or end—nor expiration date.
- Jacqueline Pirtle

How does the phrase "The End" feel to you? Is there a conflict between liking it and not liking it? Why do you think you actually truly think there is an end—and does that scare you? Can you shift your belief to "there is never an end" since energetically there are none? How can you convince yourself to get out of physicality - where "The End" is used in movies, books, and when death is present - and step into your infinite essence of always being something?

_____
_____
_____
_____
_____

And so it is!

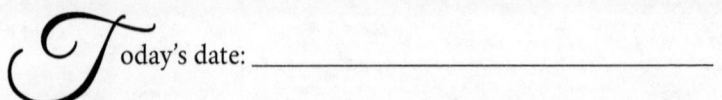oday's date: _____

Start your sentence with: "I would give anything for..." and complete it with what you want and won't be denied for today. Be clear, write with an open heart, a smile, and ecstatic excitement.

_____
_____
_____
_____
_____

Start your sentence with: "I would give anything for..." and complete it with what you want and won't be denied for your far and near future—you know, the incredible big stuff you wish for.

_____
_____
_____
_____
_____

Time for night-night gratitude! Write down what went great today by starting your sentence with: "I am grateful for..." then add the good stuff and expect a night of sweet dreams.

_____
_____
_____
_____
_____

QUOTE

Celebrate like there is no tomorrow, since this is your golden opportunity to let your hair down and turn your mind off.
- Jacqueline Pirtle

Do you like celebrating? How often, when, and how; do you prefer spontaneous or planned? What energy does celebration carry for you—how excited do you get when it is time to celebrate? Do you dress up or go as is? What belongs to a great celebration? How can you celebrate - even just energetically - at least once a day to intensify the energy of your life?

_____
_____
_____
_____
_____
_____
_____
_____

And so it is!

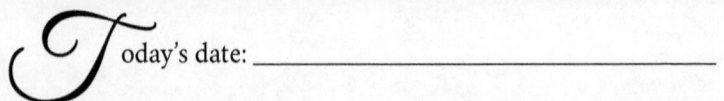
Today's date: _____

Start your sentence with: "I would give anything for…" and complete it with what you want and won't be denied for today. Be clear, write with an open heart, a smile, and ecstatic excitement.

_____
_____
_____
_____
_____

Start your sentence with: "I would give anything for…" and complete it with what you want and won't be denied for your far and near future—you know, the incredible big stuff you wish for.

_____
_____
_____
_____
_____

Time for night-night gratitude! Write down what went great today by starting your sentence with: "I am grateful for…" then add the good stuff and expect a night of sweet dreams.

_____
_____
_____
_____
_____

QUOTE

Fog trains your trust. - Jacqueline Pirtle

Pretend you are surrounded by complete fog—visibility is zero and there is nothing to see. How do you feel? Now add complete trust to that situation; trust that you are okay, that you are safe and sound, that you are guided where to go and what to do, and that at some point the fog will disappear—how do you feel now? Better? How can you base your life and how you show up more and more on trust, to eventually arrive at complete trust; trust in yourself, your inner you, the universe and consciousness?

_____
_____
_____
_____
_____
_____
_____
_____

And so it is!

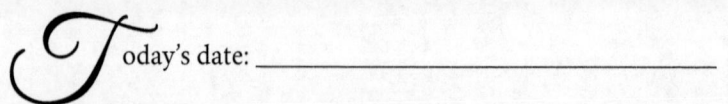

Today's date: _____

Start your sentence with: "I would give anything for..." and complete it with what you want and won't be denied for today. Be clear, write with an open heart, a smile, and ecstatic excitement.

_____
_____
_____
_____
_____

Start your sentence with: "I would give anything for..." and complete it with what you want and won't be denied for your far and near future—you know, the incredible big stuff you wish for.

_____
_____
_____
_____
_____

Time for night-night gratitude! Write down what went great today by starting your sentence with: "I am grateful for..." then add the good stuff and expect a night of sweet dreams.

_____
_____
_____
_____
_____

QUOTE

Walking backwards awakens your senses and re-programs your thinking, shifting you into creativity and playfulness. - Jacqueline Pirtle

Do you ever walk backwards, or have you seen kids walking backwards? Are you laughing and feeling funny when you do it—do you witness kids being free and playful when doing so? How can you walk backwards without feeling weird, and plan it into your daily moving around?

_____
_____
_____
_____
_____
_____
_____
_____
_____
_____

And so it is!

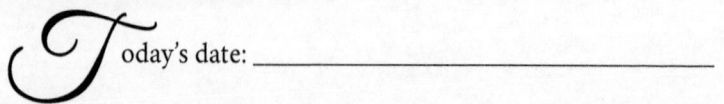oday's date: _____

START YOUR SENTENCE WITH: "I would give anything for…" and complete it with what you want and won't be denied for today. Be clear, write with an open heart, a smile, and ecstatic excitement.

_____
_____
_____
_____
_____

Start your sentence with: "I would give anything for…" and complete it with what you want and won't be denied for your far and near future—you know, the incredible big stuff you wish for.

_____
_____
_____
_____
_____

Time for night-night gratitude! Write down what went great today by starting your sentence with: "I am grateful for…" then add the good stuff and expect a night of sweet dreams.

_____
_____
_____
_____
_____

QUOTE

Opening yourself up shows that you have strength. - Jacqueline Pirtle

Do you feel that closing yourself and your heart keeps you safe? If yes, why and how does it feel that way? If not, how does being open feel to you? How can you open yourself more and more and trust that you are safe being that open—while also knowing that when you are open great things can be delivered without any restrictions?

_____
_____
_____
_____
_____
_____
_____
_____
_____
_____

And so it is!

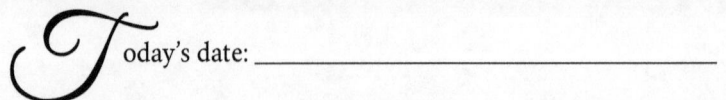 oday's date: _____

Start your sentence with: "I would give anything for…" and complete it with what you want and won't be denied for today. Be clear, write with an open heart, a smile, and ecstatic excitement.

_____
_____
_____
_____
_____

Start your sentence with: "I would give anything for…" and complete it with what you want and won't be denied for your far and near future—you know, the incredible big stuff you wish for.

_____
_____
_____
_____
_____

Time for night-night gratitude! Write down what went great today by starting your sentence with: "I am grateful for…" then add the good stuff and expect a night of sweet dreams.

_____
_____
_____
_____
_____

QUOTE

Surroundings and environments matter, because they either make you or break you. - Jacqueline Pirtle

What is your environment, your surroundings? Are they making you or breaking you? Could you change them or make them better, or remove yourself to a better situation? How much are you contributing to a good environment—or how much to a bad one? What environments are good for you to prosper and thrive? How can you create better for yourself?

_____
_____
_____
_____
_____
_____
_____
_____
_____

And so it is!

BONUS

Because hey, nobody ever wants these brilliant manifestations to end.

So keep on "I'd Give Anything For-ing" because there is never a ceiling to what's possible.

*T*oday's date: _____

M*Y* DEEPEST WISHES **and dreams are:**

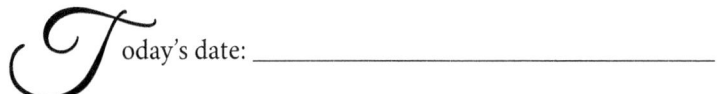
Today's date: _____

MY MOST BEAUTIFUL HOPES ARE:

_____
_____
_____
_____
_____
_____
_____
_____
_____
_____
_____
_____
_____
_____
_____
_____
_____
_____
_____
_____
_____
_____
_____
_____
_____
_____
_____
_____

Today's date: _____

I LOVE IT WHEN:

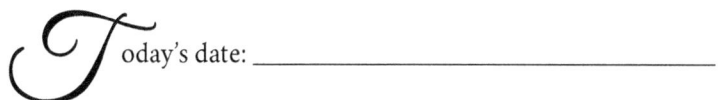Today's date: _____

LIFE IS BEST WHEN:

Today's date: _____

I FEEL MY BEST WHEN:

_____
_____
_____
_____
_____
_____
_____
_____
_____
_____
_____
_____
_____
_____
_____
_____
_____
_____
_____
_____
_____
_____
_____
_____

* * *

Don't forget to leave a review on Amazon.com and Goodreads.com as soon as you can, as your kind feedback helps other readers find my books easier. Thank you!

I truly hope your brilliant wishes came true and that you enjoyed *I'd Give Anything For...* as much as I loved writing it.

To find out more about my work and books check out:

www.freakyhealer.com
My Amazon Author Page (Jacqueline Pirtle)

ABOUT THE AUTHOR

Jacqueline Pirtle is an internationally-renowned Mindful Happiness expert and the bestselling author of over 16 transformational personal growth books for adults and children.

She is a thought leader in the fields of mindfulness, happiness, energy work, spirituality, energetic living and businessing, wholesome healing, and the teachings of one's soul.

Jacqueline has over 28 years of experience and has helped thousands of clients all over the world to discover their own happiness and how to live a conscious and mindfully aligned life filled with health, happiness, abundance, and success.

As the owner of *FreakyHealer* she has shared her solid teachings through her bestselling books, podcasts **The Weekly Freak** *&* **The Corporate Happiness Show**, sessions, workshops, courses and programs, talks and presentations with clients worldwide. She holds international degrees in holistic health and natural living, is certified for hypnosis sessions for PTSD, and is a Reiki Master.

Her highly effective healing work has been featured in print and online magazines, podcasts, radio shows, on TV, and in the documentaries **The Overly Emotional Child** **by** **Learning Success**, available on *Amazon Prime*, and Hacking Happiness.

For any questions you might have, to sign up for Jacqueline's newsletter, and for more information on whatever else she is up to, visit www.freakyhealer.com and her social media accounts @freakyhealer.

f X ◉

www.ingramcontent.com/pod-product-compliance
Lightning Source LLC
LaVergne TN
LVHW011158050225
803025LV00006B/194